HOME-STYLE CHINESE COOKING

HOME-STYLE

CHINESE COOKING

MAIN DISHES • RICE & NOODLES • SOUPS • DESSERTS

TSUNG-YUN WAN

Marshall Cavendish Cuisine

Editor: Melissa Tham
Designer: Benson Tan
Photographer: Chris Radley of Chris Radley Photography (chrisradleyphotography.com)
Illustrator: Liv Wan of Liv Wan Illustration (livwanillustration.com)

Published by Marshall Cavendish Cuisine
An imprint of Marshall Cavendish International

Other Marshall Cavendish Offices:
Marshall Cavendish Corporation. 99 White Plains Road, Tarrytown NY 10591-9001, USA • Marshall Cavendish International (Thailand) Co Ltd. 253 Asoke, 12th Flr, Sukhumvit 21 Road, Klongtoey Nua, Wattana, Bangkok 10110, Thailand • Marshall Cavendish (Malaysia) Sdn Bhd, Times Subang, Lot 46, Subang Hi-Tech Industrial Park, Batu Tiga, 40000 Shah Alam, Selangor Darul Ehsan, Malaysia

National Library Board, Singapore Cataloguing-in-Publication Data

Name(s): Wan, Tsung-Yun. | Radley, Chris, photographer.
Title: Home-style Chinese cooking / Tsung-Yun Wan ; photographer, Chris Radley.
Other titles: Chinese cooking
Description: Singapore : Marshall Cavendish Cuisine, [2016]
Identifier(s): OCN 954105949 | ISBN 978-981-47-5100-1 (paperback)
Subject(s): LCSH: Cooking, Chinese. | Cookbooks.
Classification: DDC 641.5951--dc23

Printed by Times Offset (M) Sdn Bhd

DEDICATION

To everyone who helped us during the development of this book. Without your help, this book would not have been possible.

CONTENTS

SEAFOOD

Cockle Meatballs 泥蚶肉丸 68

Deep-fried Prawn Balls with Almond Flakes 杏仁蝦球 70

Pineapple Prawns 鳳梨蝦球 72

Stir-fried Cashew and Prawns 腰果蝦仁 75

Prawn Fried Rice 蝦仁炒飯 76

Garlic Sauce and Vermicelli Noodles with Steamed Scallops 蒜茸粉絲蒸扇貝 78

Prawn and Passion Fruit Salad 百香果蝦仁沙拉 80

Stir-fried Jumbo Prawns in Spicy Sauce 干燒大蝦 82

Steamed Razor Clams with Black Beans and Chilli Sauce 香辣豆豉蒸蟶子 84

Squid Stuffed with Savoury Sticky Rice 糯米釀鮮魷 86

Sweet and Sour Fish Fillet 糖醋魚柳 88

VEGETABLES

Chinese Cabbage and Chive Flower Salad 涼拌白菜心 92

Stir-fried Garlic Sprouts with Bean Curd 蒜苔炒豆干 94

Lotus Root Salad 涼拌蓮藕 96

Cucumber Stuffed with Steamed Taro Mash 芋泥蒸黃瓜 98

Chinese Eggplants in Garlic and Chilli Sauce 涼拌茄子 100

Deep-fried Tofu Coated with Black Sesame 黑芝麻炸豆腐 103

Cucumber and Wood Ear Salad 涼拌黃瓜木耳 104

Kung Pao Tofu 宮保豆腐 106

Stir-fried Bitter Melon with Dried Prawns 蝦米炒苦瓜 108

SOUPS

DESSERTS

INTRODUCTION

We've all eaten food from Chinese takeaways and we've all eaten in Chinese restaurants, or at least different countries' interpretation of Chinese food but what do Chinese people really eat at home? How similar or different is it to what the West interprets as Chinese food?

When I moved to the United Kingdom in the mid 2000s, I was naturally keen to try out the local foods but I also wanted to eat the food I ate at home when I was a child. What I found in the majority of cities I went to in the UK was that there was a lot of Cantonese-style Chinese food but very little real Chinese food, the kind of food Chinese people eat in their homes. So a couple of years after I moved here, I started my blog Egg Wans Food Odyssey which is an ever-growing collection of not only recipes I've learnt from friends in the West, but also foods I ate during my childhood in Taiwan.

You might wonder how someone from Taiwan can be as knowledgeable as to write a book about Chinese food. Well, my grandparents who raised me were Chinese and every day I was surrounded by the most delicious native Chinese foods, Chinese food that we eat in our homes. I also lived in China for a period of time.

This is my third cook book and my second with Marshall Cavendish. My first focused on home-styled Taiwanese cooking and while Taiwanese and Chinese cuisine are very similar, they still have enough differences to merit writing two books about both countries' beautiful cuisines. I hope you enjoy cooking dishes from this book and remember this is the real thing that we eat in China.

TSUNG-YUN WAN

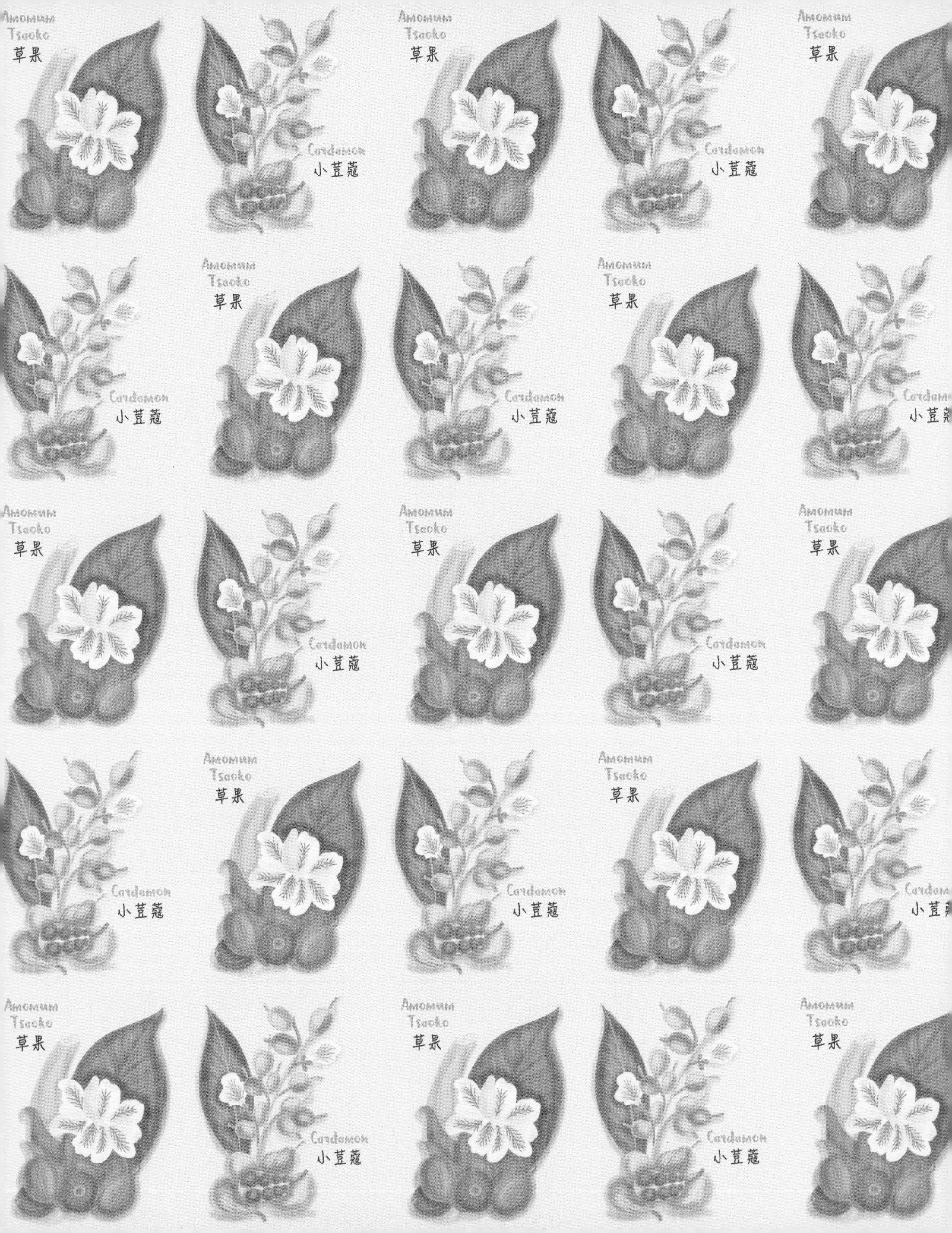
Amomum
Tsaoko
草果
Cardamon
小荳蔻

MEAT

BEEF CHOW MEIN 牛肉炒麵

Serves 3–4

Chinese *chow mein* is a really popular dish in Chinese cooking and there are many different ways to cook this dish. You can have a seafood *chow mein*, pork *chow mein*, beef, chicken or whatever you really fancy. *Chow mein* is also a very easy, delicious and healthy dish.

600 g (1 lb $5^1/_3$ oz) sirloin steak, cut into fine strips

300 g (11 oz) egg noodles

Cooking oil, as needed

1 Tbsp finely chopped ginger

3 cloves garlic, peeled and finely chopped

1 chilli, finely chopped

1 (160 g) ($5^1/_3$ oz) red bell pepper or bell pepper of desired colour

110 g ($3^1/_2$ oz) carrot, peeled and julienned

150 g ($5^1/_3$ oz) broccoli, washed and halved

Marinade

1 Tbsp rice wine

3 Tbsp light soy sauce

$^1/_2$ Tbsp sugar

$^1/_4$ tsp ground black pepper

$^1/_2$ tsp salt

$^1/_2$ tsp potato starch or cornflour

1 Tbsp water

1 tsp dark soy sauce

$^1/_4$ tsp baking soda (optional)

Seasoning

1 Tbsp oyster sauce

1 tsp salt

1 Tbsp light soy sauce

$^1/_4$ tsp blended sesame oil

1. Marinate the beef with the ingredients for the marinade for 30 minutes.
2. Boil a pot of water and cook the egg noodles until al dente. Drain, then place the noodles in cold water to cool. Drain. Toss noodles in some oil to prevent the noodles from sticking. Set aside.
3. Heat a wok with 1 Tbsp oil over medium heat. Stir-fry the beef for 30 seconds. Remove from heat and transfer to a bowl or plate.
4. Rinse the wok and heat 1 Tbsp oil over medium heat. Stir-fry the ginger, garlic and chilli for 30 seconds.
5. Add the bell pepper and carrot and stir-fry for 2–3 minutes.
6. Add the egg noodles and stir-fry for another 2 minutes, then add the seasoning. Stir-fry the noodles and toss well for another 2–3 minutes.
7. Return the beef to the wok. Stir-fry for 2–3 minutes.
8. Dish out. Garnish as desired and serve.

PEARL MEATBALLS 珍珠丸子

Makes 16–18 balls

This is a dish you can prepare the night before and all you need to do is steam it before serving. It's a delicious and beautiful dish that's very suitable for banquets and special events. Mix the mixture the same way for 2–3 minutes, either clockwise or anti-clockwise but do note that it must be consistent as this will improve the texture of the mixture.

450 g (1 lb) fatty minced pork (30% fat and 70% lean)

2 dried shiitake mushrooms, soaked in hot water to soften then finely chopped

½ Tbsp finely chopped ginger

70 g (2½ oz) finely chopped carrot

1 egg

170 g (6 oz) short-grained glutinous rice, soaked in water for a few hours

Seasoning

1 Tbsp light soy sauce

½ Tbsp potato starch

1 tsp salt

2 tsp castor sugar

Garnish

Wolfberries (goji berries)

Green herbs

1. Place all the ingredients apart from glutinous rice into a mixing bowl and add the seasoning. Mix well in an anti-clockwise direction for 2–3 minutes.
2. Separate the meat mixture and shape into small balls.
3. Coat the meat balls with glutinous rice.
4. Using a bamboo steamer, steam the meatballs for 12–15 minutes over high heat.
5. Garnish with goji berries and green herbs and serve.

Soak the sticky rice for a few hours and drain the water before coating the meatballs.

TURNIP CAKE 蘿蔔糕

Makes 5–6 turnip cakes

Chinese turnip cake is one of the most popular dishes in dim sum and is a must-have dish for Chinese New Year. Daikon is the main ingredient we use for this dish as daikon means "lucky". I used gammon steak in this recipe as it can be found in local supermarkets, while it might be quite difficult to get hold of Chinese ham. I always wait for the turnip cakes to cool down before using cling wrap to wrap the turnip cake and the tin foil box, and store it in the refrigerator. You can store the turnip cakes for up to a month but do cook it immediately once it has defrosted.

450 g (1 lb) long grain Thai rice, soaked in 600 (20¼ fl oz) water for at least 6 hours or overnight

Water, as needed

250 g (9 oz) minced pork

120 g (4⅓ oz) rice flour

Cooking oil, as needed

2 banana shallots, peeled and finely chopped

3 cloves garlic, peeled and finely chopped

3 shiitake mushrooms

30 g (1 oz) dried prawns, soaked in hot water to soften then drained and finely chopped.

200 g (7 oz) Gammon steak or Chinese ham, diced

1 kg (2 lb 3 oz) shredded daikon

Marinade

1½ Tbsp light soy sauce

1 tsp castor sugar

½ tsp salt

½ tsp five-spice powder

Seasoning for Minced Garnish

2 Tbsp light soy sauce

1 tsp castor sugar

½ tsp salt

¼ tsp ground white pepper

Daikon Seasoning

1 tsp salt

1 tsp castor sugar

1. Using a smoothie machine or blender, blend soaked rice and water until it looks like soy milk. You can add a little bit of water to aid blending if you find the rice has absorbed too much water overnight.
2. Marinate the minced pork with the ingredients for the marinade for 30 minutes.
3. Add the rice flour to blended rice and mix well to ensure that there are no lumps. Set aside.
4. Heat some oil in a wok over medium heat. Stir-fry the banana shallots and garlic until fragrant.
5. Add the shiitake mushrooms and dried prawns, then stir-fry for 2–3 minutes.
6. Add the minced pork, gammon steak or Chinese ham and the seasoning from the minced garnish. Stir-fry for a few more minutes until minced pork is thoroughly cooked. Remove from the heat. Transfer the minced pork to a plate and set aside.

7. Using the same wok, heat a little more oil and cook the daikon with the seasoning until it is soft and moisture is released. Add minced pork and mix evenly.
8. Combine the rice mixture with the daikon and reduce heat. Keep stirring until the mixture looks like a paste. Turn off heat. If you feel the mixture is a little dry or too solid, you can add some water.
9. Grease 5–6 aluminium disposable boxes, measuring 15 x 10 cm (6 x 4 in) with oil. Pour the rice cake mix into the tin box.
10. Use a steamer to steam the rice cakes. Once the water is boiling under the steamer, steam for around 45 minutes.
11. Allow the rice cakes to cool down completely before removing from the tin. Slice turnip cake into 1-cm (1/2-in) slices.
12. Heat a little oil in a frying pan over medium heat. Fry the turnip cakes until golden brown on both sides.
13. Serve with light soy sauce.

If the moisture from the daikon is not released, the quality of the turnip cake could be affected.

CHAR SIU PORK 叉燒肉

Serves 4

I always make a big portion of *char siu* pork as you can do a lot of things with this dish, including making a delicious fried rice like Yangzhou fried rice or even a delicious *chow mein*.

1 kg (2 lb 3 oz) pork shoulder, cut into long thick slices

Marinade

2 Tbsp rice wine

3 Tbsp light soy sauce

2 Tbsp demerara sugar

3 Tbsp maltose syrup

1/2 tsp salt

4 cloves garlic, peeled and sliced

2 Tbsp hoisin sauce

1 star anise

1 dried tangerine peel

1/2 tsp blended sesame oil

2 Tbsp oyster sauce

1. Place the ingredients for the marinade in a large container. Using gloved hands, massage the marinade into the pork shoulder until fully marinated.
2. Cling wrap container and place in the refrigerator. You are advised to marinate the pork for 3 days and massage marinade into the pork shoulder once a day.
3. Preheat the oven to 200°C (400°F). Remove the pork from the refrigerator and place on a roasting tray.
4. Roast the pork for 20–30 minutes, brushing the pork with marinade 3–4 times during the roasting.
5. Serve immediately.

STEAMED PORK WITH RICE POWDER

粉蒸肉

Serves 4

This is a dish that my whole family absolutely loves. In fact my husband likes it so much that whenever I ask him what he wants to eat, he will definitely say *fen jen ro* more than 50% of the time. It may require 2–3 hours of steaming, but trust me, the flavour of this dish is amazing and more than makes up for it.

1 kg (2 lb 3 oz) pork belly

170 g (6 oz) *jen ro fen* powder ("蒸肉粉") + more as needed

170 g (6 oz) sweet potatoes, peeled and cut into 1-cm (1/2-in) thick slices

Marinade

1/2 Tbsp chilli bean sauce

3 Tbsp light soy sauce

1 Tbsp rice wine

1 Tbsp demerara sugar

1/4 tsp five-spice powder

1/2 tsp sweet bean sauce

1/2 tsp dark soy sauce

1. Clean the pork belly. Boil a large pot of water and blanch the pork belly briefly to remove any impurities. Drain and rinse immediately with cold water. Pat dry and slice the pork belly into 5-cm (2-in) wide and 1-cm (1/2-in) thick sections.
2. Marinate the pork belly with the ingredients for the marinade for 30 minutes.
3. Coat the pork belly with *jen ro fen* powder. Set aside.
4. Prepare a 21.5 cm (8.5 in) wide bamboo steamer or a heatproof bowl that is of a similar size. Line the steamer or bowl with parchment paper.
5. Place a layer of sweet potato on the bottom of the bamboo steamer then layer the rest of the bamboo steamer with pork belly. You can also do 1 layer sweet potato then 1 layer pork belly on top of the sweet potato. Sprinkle *jen ro fen* powder on top and cover with the bamboo steamer lid.
6. Place a steam rack in a wok. Add 1 litre (32 fl oz / 4 cups) of water into the wok. Bring water to a boil over low heat. Place bamboo steamer in the wok and cover with lid. Steam for 2 hours over medium heat. Check occasionally to make sure there is always water in the bottom of the wok.
7. Serve warm.

This is a type of rice powder which is only used for this kind of dish. The rice powder used for rice balls or other dishes is completely different.

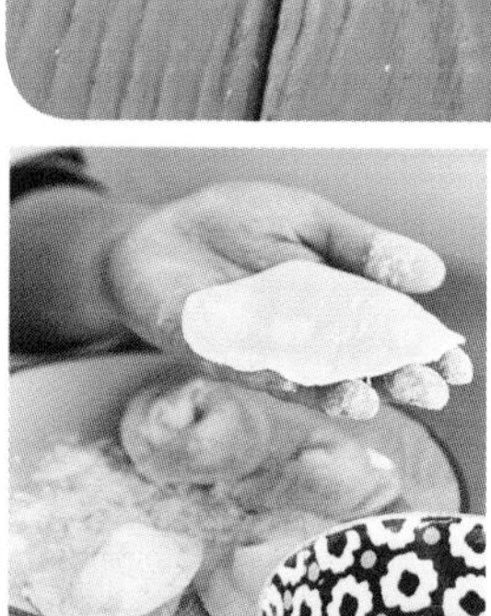

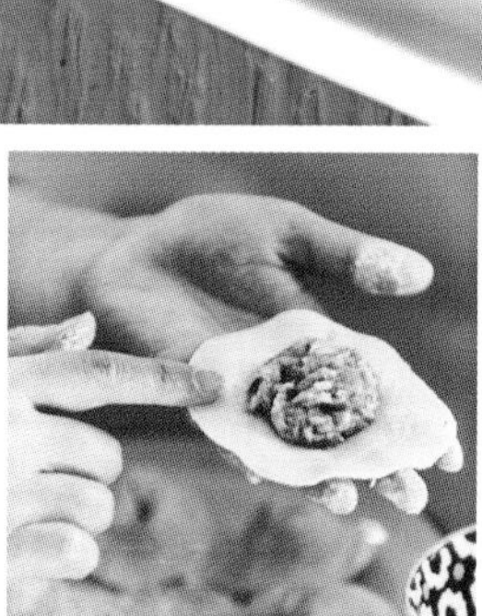
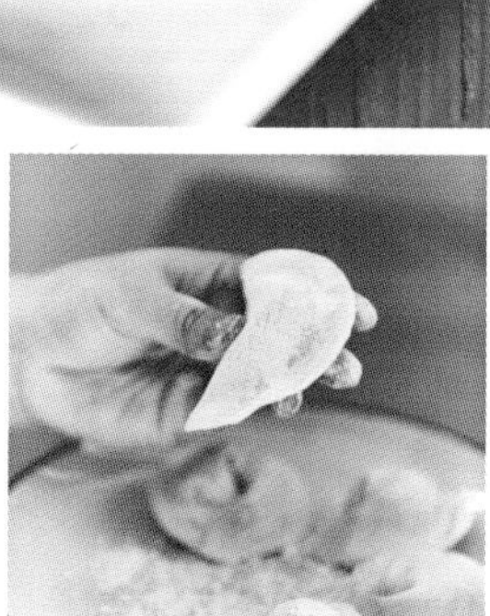
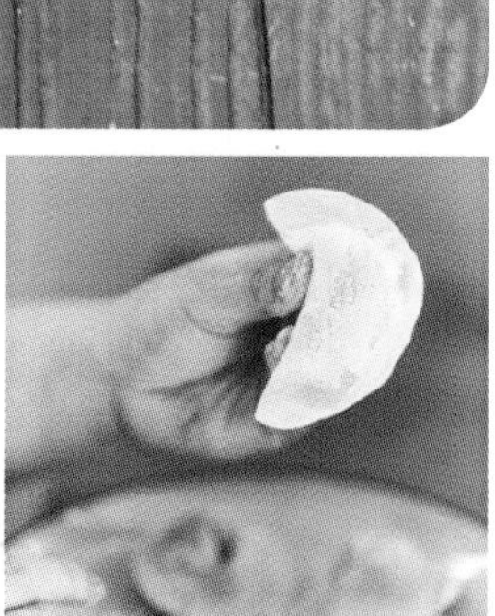

FRIED DUMPLINGS 煎餃

Makes 100–120 dumplings

The classic way of preparing dumplings is to boil them. In certain parts of China, doing anything other than boiling can be a little controversial but my family and I prefer to fry dumplings (once they are boiled) as the pastry is crisp and tastes better. If you make many dumplings, you can store them in the refrigerator. Simply cover a plate with flour, place in your refrigerator and wait until the dumplings are frozen. Transfer the dumplings into freezer bags and store. Whenever you want to eat dumplings, simply take a bag out of your refrigerator and cook as this recipe shows.

1 kg (2 lb 3 oz) minced pork

2 bunches spring onions, finely chopped

3 thin pieces of ginger, finely chopped

6 large eggs, beaten and seasoned with 1 tsp soy sauce, 1/2 tsp salt and 1 tsp demerara sugar

1 Tbsp dried prawns, softened in hot water and finely chopped

Cooking oil, as needed

Plain flour, as needed

100–120 ready-made dumpling skins

Seasoning

250 ml (8 fl oz / 1 cup) light soy sauce

1 tsp salt

1 Tbsp demerara sugar

1 Tbsp sesame oil

1. Fry the eggs as thin as a crepe and set aside to cool. When cool enough to handle, chop the eggs up finely.
2. Mix all the ingredients and the seasoning except for oil and flour well in a bowl. Set aside for 30 minutes.
3. Prepare the dumplings. Prepare a bowl of cold water at the side. You can use a little bit of water to help the edge of the dumpling pastries to stick together.
4. Place 1 tsp of filling in the centre of the dumpling skin. Dip the tips of your finger in some water and wet the two opposite ends of the pastry skin. Gently press the two ends together.
5. Repeat until dumpling skins are all used up.
6. Lightly dust a plate with flour to prevent the dumplings from sticking to the plate. Place the dumplings on the plate.
7. Bring a big pot of water to a boil over low heat. Cook the dumplings.
8. When the dumplings have risen and are floating at the surface of the water, they are cooked (Please note that this applies to fresh dumplings only. If the dumplings are frozen, you will need to wait for the water to boil then add more water. Wait to boil again, repeat twice, then they are cooked)
9. Place the dumplings in iced water to cool down. Drain. Gently mix some oil with the dumplings to prevent them from sticking together.
10. Heat a little oil in the frying pan over medium heat. Fry the dumplings until they are golden brown on the outside.
11. Serve.

BEEF SHANK WITH SPRING ONION PANCAKE WRAP 牛肉捲餅

Serves 4

This dish originates from Northern China. Northern Chinese cuisine uses flour based products as one of the main ingredients in their diet. Products like mantou, noodles and pancakes of course use flour and these are very common in Northern China. Traditionally, Chinese people use spring onions as the main vegetable in this dish but if you feel that the taste of the spring onion is too strong, you can use cucumber, pepper or some salad leaves instead.

Stewed Beef Shank

800 g (1³/₄ lb) beef shank

Cooking oil, as needed

2 spring onions, cut into 3-cm (1¹/₄-in) lengths

4 thin slices ginger

5 cloves garlic, peeled and sliced

2 shallots, peeled and roughly chopped

1 dried chilli or fresh chilli

1 Tbsp chilli bean sauce

Seasoning

1 Chinese spice bag

1 tsp fennel seeds

250 ml (8 fl oz / 1 cup) light soy sauce

1 Tbsp rice wine

1 Tbsp demerara sugar

Spring Onion Pancake

300 g (11 oz) plain flour

300 g (11 oz) bread flour

1 tsp salt + more as needed

1¹/₂ tsp demerara sugar

400 ml (13¹/₂ fl oz) warm water

70 g (2¹/₂ oz) lard or shortening

6 spring onions, finely chopped

1 Tbsp white sesame seeds

1. Prepare the stewed beef shank. Cook the beef shank in boiling water for a few minutes and rinse under cold water. Set aside.
2. Heat the oil in a wok over medium heat. Stir-fry the spring onions, ginger, garlic, shallots, chilli until fragrant. Add the chilli bean sauce and stir-fry for 30 seconds.
3. Place the beef shank and stir-fried ingredients in a stockpot. Add seasoning. Pour sufficient water into stockpot to cover the beef shank. Bring the beef shank to a boil, then simmer over low heat for 2 hours.
4. Prepare the spring onion pancake. Mix the plain flour and bread flour, salt and sugar with warm water together in a bowl. Knead until the dough is soft and smooth.
5. Cover the dough with a clean, wet tea towel and set aside for 20–30 minutes.
6. Separate the dough into 10 small dough balls and flatten them individually.
7. Brush the lard or shortening on the flattened dough and sprinkle spring onions, sesame and some salt.
8. Roll the further edge of the dough inwards to get a cylinder. Roll the dough inwards from the left to form a bun. Roll the dough into a flat disc.
9. Using a little bit of oil, fry the pancake until both sides are golden brown and crisp.
10. Slice the beef shank into thick slices and wrap them with spring onion pancakes, chilli bean sauce, spring onion or any salad vegetable you like.
11. Serve warm.

STEAMED MEATBALLS IN CHESTNUT MUSHROOM 香菇鑲肉丸

Makes 9 mushrooms

This dish is very quick and simple to make but also low in fat. It's also a really great looking dish that you can serve for special events.

240 g (8$^1/_2$ oz) minced pork
55 g (2 oz) grated carrot
1 spring onion, finely chopped
1 tsp finely chopped ginger
9 chestnut mushrooms

Seasoning

1 Tbsp light soy sauce
$^1/_2$ tsp dark soy sauce
$^1/_4$ tsp ground black pepper
$^1/_2$ tsp demerara sugar
$^1/_2$ tsp blended sesame oil
$^1/_2$ tsp salt

1. Mix all the ingredients apart from the chestnut mushrooms together in a big mixing bowl.
2. Add the seasoning and mix for a few more minutes.
3. Portion and form minced mixture into 9 small balls. Fill mushroom caps with minced meatballs. Repeat this procedure until the ingredients are used up.
4. Sandwich the meatballs in between chestnut mushrooms.
5. Steam the meatballs for 10–12 minutes over high heat.
6. Garnish as desired. Serve warm.

CHINESE BBQ RIBS 中式烤肋排

Serves 5

Chinese BBQ ribs are one of the most popular things I make at home. Almost everyone in the UK loves this dish and I receive many emails asking for a recipe for this so I decided it would be a good idea to include this recipe in the cookbook.

1 kg (2 lb 3 oz) pork ribs

100 ml (3$^1/_2$ fl oz) water

Marinade

2 Tbsp light soy sauce

1 Tbsp demerara sugar

Juice from 2 oranges

1 Tbsp honey

Dried Spices

$^1/_2$ tsp five-spice powder

$^1/_2$ tsp ground black pepper

1 tsp ground garlic

$^1/_2$ tsp ground cumin

$^1/_4$ tsp ground clove

BBQ sauce

3 Tbsp ketchup

$^1/_4$ tsp blended sesame oil

1 Tbsp sweet bean sauce

2 Tbsp marinade

1. This dish has to be prepared a day in advance.
2. Rub the dried spices all over the pork ribs and marinate overnight.
3. Marinate the ribs with the marinade for 2–3 hours.
4. Preheat oven to 150°C (300°F).
5. Prepare the BBQ sauce. Place all the ingredients for the sauce in a saucepan. Bring to a boil, then simmer over low heat for 3–5 minutes.
6. Place the ribs in a roasting tray. Add orange juice, 3–4 Tbsp marinade and water in the roasting tray.
7. Cover the roasting tray with tin foil and roast for 2–3 hours. Check tenderness of the ribs often with a skewer. If the rib is still tough and there is little liquid in the tray, add more water.
8. When the pork ribs are soft, tear tin foil away and brush the BBQ sauce on the ribs. Increase oven temperature to 170°C (338°F).
9. Brush the BBQ sauce on the ribs once every 15 minutes.
10. Remove the pork ribs from the oven. Serve.

DONGPO PORK 東坡肉

Serves 4

This is another very popular dish in Chinese cooking. Not only is it a very easy dish to make, it also looks and tastes amazing. The parcel-like presentation makes this dish very popular for Chinese banquets and special events. This pork dish was created when Su Dongpo worked and lived in Hangzhou. One day he decided to make stewed pork and one of his old friends suddenly visited him while he was cooking. He challenged Su Dongpo to a game of Chinese chess and Su Dongpo had totally forgotten he had some pork stewed on the stove. It was only when he could smell the pork coming out of his kitchen that he remembered he was cooking and it smelt amazing.
He tasted the pork and shared it with his friends and through a wonderful accident, one of the most popular dishes in Chinese cuisine emerged.

1.5 kg (3 lb 4½ oz) pork belly

Cooking oil, as needed

5 cloves garlic, peeled and sliced

3 spring onions, sliced into 3-cm (1¼-in) lengths

3 slices ginger

1 dried tangerine peel

2 licorice roots

1 star anise

5-cm (2-in) cinnamon stick

Seasoning

125 ml (4 fl oz / ½ cup) light soy sauce

1 Tbsp dark soy sauce

100 g (3½ oz) rock sugar

90 ml (3 fl oz / ⅜ cup) rice wine or Shaoxing rice wine

625 ml (20 fl oz / 2½ cups) water

1. Clean the pork belly. Boil a large pot of water and blanch the pork belly briefly to remove any impurities. Drain and rinse immediately with cold water. Pat dry and cut the pork belly into 5-cm (2-in) square cubes and tie the cubes with string to look like a parcel.
2. Heat some oil in a wok over medium heat. Place the pork belly skin side down and cover the lid. Fry the pork belly until the skin turns golden. Please be very careful with this procedure as the pork skin will cause the oil to splatter. If you would like to check on the pork skin, do take note to turn the heat down before checking.
3. Heat a little bit of oil in a stockpot over medium heat and stir-fry the garlic, spring onions, ginger and all the spices for 30 seconds. Add water and seasoning and bring to a boil.
4. Lower the heat and add the pork belly. Bring back to a boil, then lower the heat and simmer for 1.5–2 hours.
5. Check if the pork belly cubes are nice and soft. Simmer a bit longer if the meat is still slightly tough. If the sauce is too watery, allow it to reduce down slightly to thicken.
6. Dish out. Serve the pork belly with rice and vegetables.

STEAMED CABBAGE ROLLS WITH MINCED PORK 白菜佛手

Makes 12–14 rolls

This dish in Chinese is "白菜佛手". 佛手 means Buddha's hand in Chinese and I think the reason people call this dish Buddha's hand is because the Chinese cabbage roll looks like a hand on the plate. Chinese cabbage leaves are very healthy, high in nutrition and also incredibly low in calories. One of the scientific studies I read suggests the antioxidant plant compounds in Chinese cabbage can help to protect the human body against breast, colon and prostate cancers and help reduce low-density lipoprotein (LDL) or so called "bad cholesterol" levels in the blood.

300 g (11 oz) minced pork

12–14 Chinese cabbage

2 spring onions, finely chopped

1 Tbsp finely chopped ginger

1 Tbsp dried prawns, softened in the warm water and finely chopped

Seasoning

1 Tbsp light soy sauce

1/2 Tbsp dark soy sauce

1 tsp cornflour or potato starch

1/2 Tbsp demerara sugar

1/2 tsp sesame oil

Sauce

1 tsp cornflour or potato starch

1 Tbsp water

1/2 Tbsp oyster sauce

2 Tbsp stock from cooking steamed Chinese cabbage rolls

1. Cut the root part of the Chinese cabbage off and rinse under cold water.
2. Bring a big pot of water to a boil over low heat. Blanch the Chinese cabbage leaves.
3. Mix minced pork, spring onions, ginger, dried prawns and seasoning in a bowl and set aside for 30 minutes.
4. Trim the Chinese leaves to form a rectangle.
5. Place 1 Tbsp of minced pork mixture on the bottom of the cabbage leaf and roll upwards until the filling is firmly wrapped.
6. Place the cabbage leaf rolls on a heatproof plate and steam for 10 minutes over high heat.
7. Prepare the sauce. Place the seasoning in a saucepan and mix evenly until there are no lumps.
8. Bring sauce to a boil over low heat. Cook until it thickens. Place the cabbage leaf rolls on a serving plate. Pour the sauce over.
9. Serve.

PAN-FRIED STUFFED LOTUS ROOT
蓮藕夾肉

Makes 9–10 stuffed lotus roots

One of the questions I often get asked by my blog readers is "how do you cook lotus root?". There are many different ways to prepare this delicious vegetable and this recipe, which is one of my personal favourites, is just one example. Incidentally this dish looks like a healthy version of a burger.

370 g (13 oz) fatty minced pork (30% fat and 70% lean)

1 spring onion, finely chopped

2 lotus roots, peeled and sliced into 0.5-cm (1/5-in) rounds

1 egg

1 Tbsp potato starch

Cooking oil, as needed

Seasoning

1 Tbsp demerara sugar

1 tsp salt

2 Tbsp light soy sauce

1/4 tsp ground black pepper

1 Tbsp potato starch or cornflour

Seasoning for Sauce

1 Tbsp oyster sauce

1 Tbsp demerara sugar

1/2 tsp potato starch or cornflour

2 Tbsp water

1 Tbsp light soy sauce

90 ml (3 fl oz / 3/8 cup) water

1. Mix the minced pork, spring onion, egg and the seasoning in a mixing bowl.
2. Portion the minced pork mixture into 10 balls.
3. Sprinkle the potato starch on one side of the lotus root. Place a ball of minced pork on a piece of lotus root. Run potato starch along the sides of the lotus root. Top with another piece of lotus root. Gently press the two pieces of lotus root together and make sure that the minced pork and lotus root stick together.
4. Heat some oil in a frying pan and pan-fry both sides of the lotus root until golden. Please be gentle when you flip the lotus root because you do not want the lotus root separating from the minced pork.
5. Add all the seasoning for sauce in a bowl. Mix well to ensure that there are no lumps.
6. Add the seasoning into the frying pan. Bring ingredients to a boil over low heat. Lower the heat and simmer to thicken the sauce.
7. Dish out. Garnish as desired and serve.

SHANGHAI-STYLE SWEET AND SOUR PORK RIBS 上海糖醋小排

Serves 4

This dish was one of my favourite dishes when I was young. I'm not a big fan of Cantonese-style sweet and sour as I feel that the ketchup used makes it too heavy and too rich. I like Cantonese-style sweet and sour fish fillet but I've just never liked ketchup-based sweet and sour sauce with pork. I always remember the first time my grandfather made this dish for me. I was thrilled and shocked at how tasty this dish is. The black vinegar tastes so different compared to rice vinegar. The acidity is a lot more mellow. My grandfather was the kind of person who would cook the same thing over and over again once you mentioned that you liked the dish. As a result, I ate this dish many times when I was a child.

700 g (1½ lb) pork ribs, cut into 3–4-cm (1¼–1½-in) long sections

500 ml (16 fl oz / 2 cups) cooking oil

1 tsp white sesame seeds, for garnish

Marinade

2 tsp salt

1 Tbsp rice wine

1 egg white

½ Tbsp potato starch or cornflour

1 Tbsp plain flour

¼ tsp ground white pepper

Seasoning

180 ml (6 fl oz / ¾ cup) water

100 g (3½ oz) demerara sugar

2 Tbsp light soy sauce

60 ml (2 fl oz / ¼ cup) black vinegar

1. Marinate the ribs with salt and rice wine for at least 30 minutes.
2. Add the egg white, potato starch or cornflour, plain flour and ground white pepper. Mix well.
3. Heat the oil in a wok or deep saucepan over medium heat, fry the ribs for 3–4 minutes until golden brown.
4. Remove the ribs from the wok. Drain the oil. Transfer the ribs to a plate with clean kitchen towels to remove excess oil.
5. Place water and sugar into a wok and cook until the syrup has caramelized.
6. Return the ribs to the wok and stir-fry for 3–4 minutes. Mix the ribs well until they are generously coated with the syrup.
7. Add the light soy sauce and cook for a few minutes.
8. Add the black vinegar and stir-fry for a few minutes.
9. Garnish with white sesame seeds.
10. Serve warm.

STIR-FRIED BASIL AND MUSHROOM PORK BELLY 塔香五花肉

Serves 4

You can use pork belly with or without skin. It's entirely up to you. But please be careful when you fry the pork belly because the pork skin can cause the oil to splatter. For this reason I always cook the pork with the lid on. This dish is a perfect dish for busy week days as you can serve it with some rice. You get all the nutrition you need so you don't need to cook a whole table's worth of food. This dish is also one of my family's favourite recipes.

700 g ($1^{1}/_{2}$ lb) pork belly

Cooking oil, as needed

10 thin slices ginger

110 g (4 oz) wood ear, julienned (This weight is after the wood ear have been softened in the water.)

160 g ($5^{1}/_{3}$ oz) mixed mushrooms

1 chilli, seeded and julienned

A handful of Thai basil leaves or western basil leaves

Seasoning

125 ml (4 fl oz / $^{1}/_{2}$ cup) light soy sauce

1 Tbsp dark soy sauce

1 Tbsp demerara sugar

2 Tbsp rice wine

90 ml (3 fl oz / $^{3}/_{8}$ cup) water

$^{1}/_{2}$ tsp sesame oil

1. Clean the pork belly. Pat dry and cut into thin strips.
2. Heat a little oil in a non-stick wok or frying pan over medium heat. Fry the pork belly until golden brown.
3. Remove the pork belly from the wok. Fry ginger with the remaining oil until the ginger is dry and curls up. Be careful not to burn the ginger as it can leave a bitter taste to the dish.
4. Add the wood ear and mixed mushrooms to the wok. Stir-fry for 1 minute. Add the chilli and the seasoning except for the sesame oil.
5. Bring the ingredients to a boil. Once boiled, lower to medium heat and reduce the liquid in the wok until it is nearly dry.
6. Add the Thai basil leaves or western basil leaves and sesame oil. Mix well and turn off heat.
7. Dish out. Garnish as desired and serve.

Note: The pork belly would have generated quite a bit of oil to fry the ginger so there is no need to add more oil.

SPICY GARLIC ROASTED LAMB CHOPS
香辣蒜香烤羊排

Serves 3

Originally I was planning on "deep-frying" this dish but for health purposes, I decided to roast the lamb instead. Some people like this fried, some roasted but using this method requires less oil and you still get a crispy, juicy and delicious lamb chop.

700 g (1½ lb) rack of lamb
Cooking oil, as needed
½ Tbsp finely chopped ginger
55 g (2 oz) finely chopped garlic
3 dried chillies, roughly diced
45 g (1½ oz) panko bread crumbs
1 tsp salt
1 small egg, beaten

Seasoning
1 Tbsp light soy sauce
½ Tbsp dark soy sauce
½ tsp ground cumin
¼ ground black pepper
1 tsp salt

1. Marinate the lamb with all the ingredients for the seasoning apart from salt for 30 minutes.
2. Heat 2 Tbsp oil in a small saucepan over medium heat. Fry the ginger, garlic and dried chillies until the garlic is lightly golden. Be careful not to burn it. Reserve the oil.
3. Mix the fried ginger, garlic, chillies and reserved oil with the panko bread crumbs. Season with 1 tsp salt.
4. Heat 1 Tbsp of oil in a frying pan over medium heat. Sear the lamb slightly. Remove from heat. Set aside to rest for a few minutes.
5. Coat the lamb with egg, then coat with the bread crumbs.
6. Preheat oven to 180°C (350°F).
7. Place the lamb chop on a roasting tray and cover the tray with tin foil. Roast for 10 minutes. Remove the tin foil and roast for another 5–8 minutes until the bread crumbs are golden.
8. Serve with salad leaves.

XIAN LAMB KEBAB 西安羊肉串

Serves 5

Before my husband and I got married, we spent some time travelling around China. One of our favourite places was Xian with it's amazing history, architecture and perhaps more importantly for us, the incredible food they had there. One of our favourite things was this Xian lamb kebab. Between the two of us, we must have eaten 30–40 lamb skewers along with a soup, some bread and a few bottles of beer. That was one of our best travel memories so far. So after we moved back to the UK, I tried to create this dish at home. I believe this recipe is as close as you will get to the real thing and I'm confident you'll like it.

400 g ($14^{1}/_{3}$ oz) lamb shank, cut into 2-cm ($^{3}/_{4}$-in) pieces

$^{1}/_{2}$ onion, peeled and sliced

2 thin slices ginger, finely chopped

10–12 bamboo skewers

Seasoning

1 Tbsp ground cumin

1 tsp chilli powder

3 Tbsp light soy sauce

1 tsp salt

1 tsp sugar

$^{1}/_{4}$ tsp ground black pepper

1 Tbsp vegetable oil

1. Marinate the lamb with onion, ginger and the ingredients for seasoning for 30 minutes.
2. Preheat the oven to 200°C (400°F).
3. Soak the bamboo skewers in the cold water for at least 30 minutes.
4. Thread 5 pieces of lamb into each bamboo skewer.
5. Roast the lamb for 5 minutes then turn the oven to grill mode. Grill the lamb kebab for another 5 minutes.
6. Garnish as desired. Serve.

Note: You may also use a char-grill pan to finish cooking the kebab.

Clove
丁香
Bay Leaf
月桂葉
Clove
丁香
Bay Leaf
月桂葉
Clove
丁香
Bay Leaf
月桂葉
Clove
丁香
Bay Leaf
月桂葉
Clove
丁香
Bay Leaf
月桂葉
Clove
丁香
Bay Leaf
月桂葉
Clove
丁香
Bay Leaf
月桂葉
Clove
丁香
Bay Leaf
月桂葉
Clove
丁香
Bay Leaf
月桂葉
Clove
丁香
Bay Leaf
月桂葉
Clove
丁香
Bay Leaf
月桂葉
Clove
丁香

POULTRY

DEEP-FRIED CHICKEN WALNUT MEATBALLS 炸核桃雞球

Make 18–20 balls

Traditionally this dish was prepared with sliced chicken breast but I decided to switch things up by preparing chicken balls instead. This makes them look cuter and more fun. This is a perfect food for banquets, parties or any special events and it's very easy to make. You can also make it ahead then finish cooking it in the oven before serving.

700 g (1$^1/_2$ lb) chicken thigh fillet, diced

1 Tbsp finely chopped ginger

1 Tbsp dried prawns, soaked in hot water to soften then finely chopped

$^1/_2$ egg

1 Tbsp cornflour

2 spring onions, finely chopped

280 g (10 oz) toasted walnuts, finely chopped

750 ml (24 fl oz) cooking oil

Seasoning

1$^1/_2$ Tbsp light soy sauce

1$^1/_2$ tsp salt

$^1/_2$ Tbsp demerara sugar

$^1/_4$ tsp blended sesame oil

$^1/_4$ tsp ground white pepper

1. Using a food processor, process the chicken, ginger and dried prawns for 1 minute.
2. Add egg, cornflour and all the ingredients for seasoning and process for another 1 minute. Transfer processed ingredients to a bowl and mix with spring onions.
3. Wet both hands with some cold water and roll the chicken mixture into small balls. Repeat this procedure until all the mixture has been used up.
4. Coat the chicken balls with walnuts.
5. Heat the oil in a wok or deep saucepan and deep-fry the chicken balls for 20 seconds over medium heat. Remove the chicken balls from the wok or saucepan and drain the oil.
6. Preheat the oven to 180°C (350°F). Place a sheet of parchment paper on a roasting tray.
7. Place the chicken balls on the tray. Cover the tray with tin foil and roast for 15 minutes.
8. Serve with ketchup or sweet chilli sauce.

CHICKEN AND MUNG BEAN SHEET SALAD 雞絲拉皮

Serves 3–4

The traditional way to prepare this dish is to use chicken breast but I used chicken legs because I like the texture of the chicken legs a lot more. Crispy chicken skin is optional if you don't think it's too much trouble to prepare. I personally think crispy chicken skin gives this dish a very interesting texture. You should be able to purchase mung bean starch sheets from your local Chinese supermarket otherwise you can just serve this dish with cucumbers and carrots.

3 chicken legs (including thigh) or chicken breast, remove skin and keep for later

280 g (10 oz) mung bean starch sheet, sliced into 2-cm (3/4-in) wide sheets

1/2 cucumber, julienned

1 small carrot, peeled and julienned

Ingredients to boil Chicken

1 litre (32 fl oz / 4 cups) water

3 slices ginger

1 Tbsp Shaoxing rice wine

5–6 Sichuan peppercorns + more as needed

1 star anise

1/2 Tbsp salt

Sauce

3 Tbsp Chinese white sesame paste or tahini sauce

2 cloves garlic, peeled and chopped

1 Tbsp demerara sugar

3 Tbsp light soy sauce

1 tsp salt

1/2 Tbsp Sichuan pepper oil

1/2 Tbsp chilli oil

2 tsp rice vinegar

1 Tbsp chicken stock from cooking the chicken

1. Blanch the chicken legs or chicken breast in boiling water for a few minutes. Drain and rinse under cold water.
2. Place the water, chicken, ginger, rice wine, Sichuan peppercorns, star anise and salt into a stockpot large enough to hold all the ingredients. Bring to a boil, then simmer over low heat for 20 minutes. Make sure the water fully covers the chicken.
3. Remove the chicken legs and set aside to cool. Pull the chicken meat off the bone and tear it into small pieces with your hand. Set aside.
4. Preheat oven to 180°C (350°F). Season the chicken skin with ground Sichuan pepper and salt.
5. Place a sheet of parchment paper on a roasting tray. Place the chicken skin on the tray and flatten the chicken skin. Roast the chicken skin until crisp and chop it roughly.
6. Blanch the mung bean starch sheet in boiling water for 2 minutes. Remove from the heat. Place the mung bean starch sheet in cold water. Drain the water. Set aside.
7. Prepare the sauce. Using a food processor, process all the ingredients for the sauce for a few minutes.
8. Place the mung bean starch sheet on a serving plate then top with cucumber and carrot.
9. Place the chicken on top of carrot and cucumber then pour desired amount of amount of sauce over
10. Garnish as desired. Sprinkle the crispy chicken skin on top. Serve with cooked mung bean starch sheet.

SICHUAN-STYLE CHICKEN IN SPICY CHILLI SAUCE 四川口水雞

Serves 4

This dish has a funny Chinese name "口水雞". "口水" means saliva in Chinese so this dish is effectively called saliva chicken in Chinese. I'm not too sure why it's called saliva chicken but I believe this dish is really delicious and it makes your mouth water just thinking about it.

4–5 chicken legs (including thighs), deboned

55 g (2 oz) toasted peanuts, peeled and finely chopped

1 cucumber, peeled and julienned

Marinade

1 Tbsp rice wine

6–7 thin slices ginger

1 spring onion

1 tsp salt

Sauce

1 spring onion, finely chopped

2 cloves garlic, peeled and finely chopped

1 tsp finely chopped ginger

Seasoning

2 Tbsp Sichuan pepper oil

2 Tbsp chilli oil

$^1/_2$ tsp Chinese white sesame paste

$^1/_2$ tsp rice vinegar

2 Tbsp light soy sauce

Blended sesame oil, as needed

1 Tbsp sugar

1. Marinate the chicken legs with the ingredients for the marinade for 30 minutes.
2. Roll the chicken leg with plastic wrap individually and steam for 20–25 minutes. Set the chicken leg aside to cool down.
3. Mix all the seasoning and the sauce in a bowl. Set aside for 30 minutes.
4. Place the cucumber on a serving plate. Remove the plastic wrap from the chicken. Slice the chicken into thick slices and place on top of the cucumber.
5. Drizzle the sauce on top of the chicken and garnish with peanuts.
6. Serve.

DEEP-FRIED LYCHEE STUFFED CHICKEN WINGS 荔枝炸雞翅

Make 12–15 chicken wings

This dish is really delicious, looks great and isn't complicated to make. It's very suitable for banquets, parties and all kinds of special events. If you can't find lychee then you can use mango but I prefer the flavour of lychee with this dish.

140 g (5 oz) skinless boneless chicken breast, remove all the excess fat

12–15 chicken wings

6–8 lychees, peeled and stoned then finely chopped

2 eggs, reserve 1 egg white for mixture

750 ml (24 fl oz / 3 cups) oil

340 g (12 oz) plain flour

100 g ($3\frac{1}{2}$ oz) panko bread crumbs

Seasoning

$\frac{1}{2}$ tsp salt

$\frac{1}{2}$ Tbsp rice wine

$\frac{1}{2}$ Tbsp ice water

$\frac{1}{4}$ ground white pepper

1 egg white

1. Using a food processor, process the chicken breast, 1 egg white and the seasoning. Process until the chicken breast is finely minced.
2. Add the lychee and mix evenly.
3. Separate the chicken wings into three sections— wingettes, drumettes and tips. Run a knife along the bone that runs through the middle of the drumettes. Do it on both sides of the bone. You will have a clean view of the bone.
4. Using the edge of the knife, scrape the bone away to remove the meat from the bone. Using your thumb, push the bone away from the meat. This will leave an indentation in the meat which you can fill with ingredients.
5. Stuff the mixture into the chicken wings. Coat the chicken wings with plain flour, eggs and panko bread crumbs.
6. Heat the oil in a wok or deep saucepan to 180°C (350°F).
7. Gently place the chicken wings into the wok or saucepan and turn off the heat for 1 minute.
8. Turn the heat back on and fry the chicken wings over medium heat until the chicken wings are golden brown.
9. Serve.

OYSTER SAUCE ASPARAGUS CHICKEN ROLLS 蠔油蘆筍雞肉捲

Make 3 chicken rolls

This is one of my favourite dishes when I was young. My grandfather usually made this dish for my lunch box. If you're not a fan of asparagus, you can replace it with spring onion, carrots or green beans.

3 whole chicken legs (including thighs), deboned, reserve skin

3–6 asparagus (if the asparagus are small and thin then you will need 6, if they're larger then less but with a minimum of 3)

Cooking oil, as needed

Marinade

2 Tbsp oyster sauce

1 Tbsp rice wine

1 Tbsp demerara sugar

1/4 ground black pepper

1. Marinate the chicken with the ingredients for the marinade overnight or for at least 1 hour.
2. Use the chicken to wrap 1 or 2 asparagus.
3. Using some string, tie the chicken and asparagus rolls up together neatly.
4. Heat some oil in a frying pan over medium low heat. Pan-fry the chicken rolls until they are golden brown.
5. Preheat the oven to 190°C (370°F). Cook chicken roll in the oven for 15 minutes.
6. Take the chicken rolls out and set aside to cool before removing strings.
7. Line a sheet of plastic wrap on a sushi bamboo mat.
8. Place the chicken roll on it and roll tightly. Set aside for 10–15 minutes.
9. Slice the chicken roll into desired thickness and remove the plastic wrap.
10. Place the chicken rolls on a plate and serve.

CHINESE POACHED CHICKEN WITH SPRING ONION OIL 蔥油雞

Serves 4

I didn't learn how to make this chicken dish until I moved to the UK. My grandparents completely dominated our kitchen in Taipei when I grew up so I rarely cooked when I lived in Taiwan. After I moved to the UK, I had to cook almost everyday and most of the time, I really missed the food from home so I would just call my mother or grandmother and ask them for recipes. This is one of the recipes my grandmother taught me and I love the taste of the chicken in this recipe. It's light, delicious and you can adjust the amount of seasoning to suit your taste.

A whole chicken around 2 kg (4 lb 6 oz)

Water to cover the chicken

1 Tbsp salt

6 spring onions; 3 sliced and 3 julienned

7 slices ginger; 2 julienned

1 chilli, julienned

1 Tbsp cooking oil

1 Tbsp blended sesame oil

Sauce

1/2 Tbsp light soy sauce

1 Tbsp fish sauce

2 cloves garlic, peeled and finely chopped

1/2 Tbsp demerara sugar

1/2 tsp ground white pepper

2 Tbsp chicken stock (from cooking the chicken)

1. Take a whole chicken and a sharp knife. Pull the chicken legs outwards so the joints will pull apart. Slice between the opened joints.
2. Turn the chicken onto the side and pull the leg back to separate. Using the knife, gently slice along the joints of the bone to separate the legs from the chicken.
3. Place the chicken on the neck end with the rear pointing towards you. Follow the skin beneath the breasts and cut down. Pull the backbone away. Separate the back bone from the crown. Pull the chicken wing out so the joint will show then slice through the joint with your knife. Gently cut through the joint. Repeat the other side for the other wing.
4. The wish bone is covered by some meat so follow the edges of the bone with your knife to fully expose it. Once the wish bone is exposed, pull it out.
5. Place water, salt, sliced spring onions and ginger in a stockpot large enough to contain everything and bring to a boil. Lower the heat, then add the chicken crown and legs and bring back to a boil. Simmer over low heat for 20 minutes then turn off the heat. Leave the chicken in the stockpot for 30–40 minutes. Remove the chicken from the stockpot and place in cold or iced water immediately.
6. Mix all the ingredients for the sauce in a bowl and set aside.
7. Debone the chicken legs and chicken crown. Slice the chicken into 1.5-cm (3/4-in) thick sections. Place the chicken on a heatproof serving plate.
8. Drizzle the sauce over the chicken. Top with julienned spring onion, ginger and chilli on the chicken.
9. Heat the oil and sesame oil in a small saucepan over medium heat. Mix well.
10. Drizzle the hot oil on top of the spring onion before serving.

KUNG PAO CHICKEN 宮保雞丁

Serves 4

Kung pao chicken is a very classic example of a Chinese home-cooking dish. It's popular in restaurants and takeaways all around the world and is also known as *gong bao* chicken. *Kung pao* chicken is classic Sichuan cuisine and this dish is named after Qing Dynasty Governor Ding BaoZhen's title. Ding Baozhen was born in Guizhou, China and he especially loved to have his meat stir-fried with chilli so after living and working in Sichuan as a governor, he asked his chef to stir-fry some chicken with chilli and peanut. This is how *kung pao* chicken was created. There are many ways to cook *kung pao* chicken but this is the method I have used for many years.

600 g (1 lb $5^1/_3$ oz) chicken thigh fillet, diced

500 ml (16 fl oz / 2 cups) oil

$^1/_2$ Tbsp Sichuan peppercorns

85 g (3 oz) skinned and untoasted peanuts

5 dried chillies, halved

2 spring onions, slice into 3-cm ($1^1/_4$-in) lengths

3 cloves garlic, peeled and sliced

Marinade

2 Tbsp light soy sauce

$^1/_2$ egg

1 Tbsp cornflour or potato starch

1 Tbsp oil

Seasoning

1 tsp blended sesame oil

1 Tbsp water

1 Tbsp light soy sauce

1 Tbsp demerara sugar

2 tsp ketchup

$^1/_2$ Tbsp dark soy sauce

1 Tbsp rice wine

$^1/_2$ tsp rice vinegar

1. Marinate the chicken with the ingredients for the marinade for 30 minutes.
2. Place all the ingredients for seasoning except rice wine and rice vinegar in a small bowl and mix well. Set aside.
3. Add the oil into a wok, then add the peanuts. Fry the peanuts over medium heat.
4. Once the peanuts have started to turn golden, remove them from the wok and set aside.
5. Using the same oil, fry the chicken until the meat turns white. Drain the oil. Set the chicken aside.
6. Reserve a little oil in the wok. Stir-fry the Sichuan peppercorns until fragrant. Remove peppercorns from the wok and dispose.
7. Add the dried chillies and fry for 15 seconds. Add spring onions and garlic. Stir-fry for another 20 seconds.
8. Add the chicken and stir-fry for 20 seconds. Add the seasoning and stir-fry for 1 minute.
9. Add the rice wine and vinegar and stir-fry for 1 minute.
10. Dish out and serve.

Note: You can adjust the amount of dried chillies and Sichuan peppercorns if you want it more or less spicy.

GENERAL TSO'S CHICKEN 左宗棠雞

Serves 3

General Tso's chicken is one of the most famous Chinese dishes. People love it all over the world and it's so popular that there is even a documentary film about this super popular dish. The creator of this dish was a Taiwan-based Hunan cuisine chef called Peng Chang-Kuei who was Chiang Kai-Shek's banquet chef. He invented this dish and named it General Tso's Chicken after the famous general from the Qing Dynasty, Zuo Zongtang, who was known as General Tso in the West. General Tso was a successful general and many say lucky so Chef Peng associated his dish with the lucky meaning.

500 g (1 lb $1\frac{1}{2}$ oz) skinned chicken thigh fillets, diced into big cubes

1 litre (32 fl oz / 4 cups) sunflower oil or olive oil

2 chillies, seeded and sliced into 3-cm ($1\frac{1}{4}$-in) long sections

2 spring onions, sliced into 2–3-cm ($\frac{3}{4}$–$1\frac{1}{4}$-in) long sections

Seasoning for Chicken Thigh Fillet

1 tsp rice wine

1 Tbsp soy sauce

$\frac{1}{2}$ egg, beaten

2 tsp potato starch or cornflour

1 tsp sunflower or olive oil

Seasoning

$1\frac{1}{2}$ Tbsp ketchup

$1\frac{1}{2}$ tsp sugar

1 Tbsp light soy sauce

Dark soy sauce, as needed

1 tsp rice wine

1 Tbsp water

1 tsp rice vinegar

A few drops of sesame oil + more as needed

A pinch of ground white pepper + more as needed

1. Marinate the chicken cubes in the ingredients for chicken thigh fillet seasoning for 10–15 minutes.
2. Heat 1 litre (32 fl oz / 4 cups) oil in a wok over medium heat. Add one chicken cube at a time into the wok. Fry until the chicken turns golden brown. Drain any liquid or oil from the chicken and set aside. Please be very careful when you add the chicken into the wok just in case the oil splatters. Do not stand too close to the wok when frying the chicken.
3. Heat 1 Tbsp of oil in a wok over medium heat. Stir-fry the chillies for 20 seconds until fragrant.
4. Add the chicken into the wok and stir-fry for 10 seconds. Add the seasoning into the wok and stir-fry until the sauce reduces.
5. Add the spring onions and stir-fry for 10 seconds. Sprinkle a few drops of sesame oil and ground white pepper.
6. Dish out and serve.

Note: You can adjust the usage of sugar if you would like this recipe to be a little sweeter.

CHINESE-STYLE SMOKED DUCK SALAD 中式燻鴨沙拉

Serves 2

This dish is one of my own creations. One of my favourite things in the world is smoked duck so I created this dish with all the usual Chinese and Eastern ingredients. I was surprised that there are not many duck dishes in Chinese cooking apart from roast duck, Peking duck and duck soup I hope you like this recipe as it's my own creation and I love to prepare this dish for my family especially during the spring and summer time. It makes a great light lunch or starter in the hot summer weather.

2 duck breasts
1 sheet of tin foil
1 Tbsp plain flour
2 teabags or 2 Tbsp black tea leaves
2 Tbsp demerara sugar
Cooking oil, as needed

Marinade

1 tsp ground Sichuan peppercorn
1½ tsp salt
1 Tbsp demerara sugar

Salad

1 beef tomato, cut into 6 wedges
2 baby gem, julienned + for garnish
1 red apple
1 green apple, sliced
1 strawberry, sliced

Salad Dressing

2 Tbsp light soy sauce
1 g (⅛ oz) kombu, cut into 3 x 5-cm (1½ x 2-in)sheet
3 Tbsp water
1 tsp mirin
½ tsp salt
2 Tbsp demerara sugar
1 tsp whole grain mustard
½ Tbsp white sesame seeds
1 Tbsp rice vinegar
½ Tbsp lime juice
1 tsp blended sesame oil

1. This dish is best prepared a day in advance.
2. Prepare the salad dressing. Place soy sauce, kombu, water, mirin, salt and sugar in a small saucepan. Bring it to a boil, then simmer over low heat for 10 minutes.
3. Add the rest of the ingredients to the saucepan and simmer for another 3–4 minutes. Turn off the heat. Set salad dressing aside to cool. Store in the refrigerator after dressing has cooled down. This dressing can be kept refrigerated for 5 days.
4. Marinate the duck breast with the ingredients for the marinade for at least 1 hour.
5. Line a sheet of the tin foil in a wok and place plain flour, teabags or tea leaves and sugar on the tin foil. Break the tea bags and only use tea leaves inside of the tea bags to smoke the duck and dispose the packaging. Place a metal rack on top of the tin foil and place the duck breast on top.
6. Heat the wok over medium heat and you should start to see the smoke come out. After smoking starts, close the lid of the wok and leave the duck breast to smoke for 2–3 minutes on each side. When cool enough to handle, slice the duck breast as desired.
7. Heat a little bit of oil in a frying pan and sear the duck breast both sides until golden brown. Set aside to cool.
8. Place the duck breast in a serving plate or bowl. Serve with salad. Drizzle the salad dressing over.

Note: Marinate duck breast ideally overnight but if not, keep duck marinated for at least 1 hour.

Clove
丁香
Bay Leaf
月桂葉
Clove
丁香
Bay Leaf
月桂葉
Clove
丁香
Bay Leaf
月桂葉
Clove
丁香
Bay Leaf
月桂葉
Clove
丁香
Bay Leaf
月桂葉
Clove
丁香
Bay Leaf
月桂葉
Clove
丁香
Bay Leaf
月桂葉
Clove
丁香
Bay Leaf
月桂葉
Clove
丁香
Bay Leaf
月桂葉
Clove
丁香
Bay Leaf
月桂葉
Clove
丁香
Bay Leaf
月桂葉
Clove
丁香
Bay Leaf
月桂葉
Clove
丁香

SEAFOOD

COCKLE MEATBALL 泥蚶肉丸

Makes 14 meatballs

I first tried these cockle meatballs while I lived in Shanghai and they tasted absolutely delicious but they were too sweet. In Shanghai restaurants, they use clams (蛤) for making the meatballs and they cook it with a very sweet sauce. I remade this dish at home based on my memory of eating it in Shanghai but managed to tone down the sweetness. Cockles can be quite salty so please be careful with the seasoning.

14 cockles, shelled

250 g (9 oz) minced pork or beef

1 tsp finely chopped ginger

1 Tbsp finely chopped spring onions

1 egg white

Seasoning

1 tsp potato starch or cornflour

1 tsp sugar

1/4 tsp ground white pepper

1/4 tsp sesame oil

1/4 tsp salt

Sauce

1 Tbsp sugar

150 ml (5 fl oz) vegetable or chicken stock (page 145)

1 Tbsp oyster sauce or thick soy sauce

1 tsp potato starch, mixed with 2 Tbsp water (this is potato starch slurry. We usually use this to thicken the sauce or soup in Chinese or Taiwanese cuisine)

1. Leave the cockles to soak in water for 2 hours to get rid of any dirt and impurities.
2. Pick the cockle meat out. Reserve both the meat and the shells. Set aside.
3. Mix the minced pork or beef, ginger, spring onions, egg white and the seasoning in a large bowl. Using your hands, mix evenly in the same direction for 3–5 minutes.
4. Chop the cockles up and add to the minced mixture. Mix well. Roll the mixture into small balls and place back into the cockle shells.
5. Steam the meatballs for 7–9 minutes until the meat is cooked all the way through.
6. Place sugar, stock and oyster sauce or thick soy sauce in a small saucepan and bring to a boil. Reduce the liquid to about half the original amount.
7. Gently stir the potato starch water slurry into the sauce and keep the stove at low heat. Keep stirring while cooking and turn off the heat once the sauce starts to boil.
8. Place the cockle meatballs on a plate and pour the sauce over. Serve.

DEEP-FRIED PRAWN BALLS WITH ALMOND FLAKES 杏仁蝦球

Make 13–14 balls

This is a dish really suitable for banquets and special events. I have always loved seafood, especially prawns, and the deep-fried almond flakes are crispy and delicious. Prawns and almonds are a great combination both in terms of texture and flavour. If you put these deep-fried prawn balls together properly, they both look and taste great, making them perfect for banquets and special events. This dish is also very easy and quick to make so it would be a great dish to treat your friends and family.

120 g ($4^1/_3$ oz) fatty minced pork

380 g ($13^3/_4$ oz) prawns, peeled and deveined

70 g ($2^1/_2$ oz) onion, peeled and finely chopped

1 Tbsp finely chopped spring onions

150 g ($5^1/_3$ oz) almond flakes, roughly chopped

$^1/_2$ Tbsp potato starch or cornflour

1 egg white

625 ml (20 fl oz / $2^1/_2$ cups) oil

Seasoning

$^1/_2$ Tbsp potato starch or cornflour

$^1/_2$ tsp salt

$^1/_2$ tsp fish sauce

$^1/_2$ tsp ground white pepper

1. Using a food processor, process fatty minced pork into a paste. The minced pork should ideally be 30% fat.
2. Add the prawns to the mix and process for a further 1–2 minutes. Transfer the processed ingredients to a big bowl once the prawns and pork are finely minced.
3. Add the seasoning, onion and spring onions. Mix the mixture in a clockwise direction for 3–5 minutes. Add potato starch and egg white.
4. Arrange almond flakes on a plate. This will make it easier for the almond flakes to stick to the prawn balls.
5. Wet both hands with cold water and take a little bit of prawn mixture and roll into a ball. Repeat this procedure until all the mixture has been rolled into balls.
6. Coat the prawn balls with almond flakes.
7. Heat the oil in a wok and fry the prawn balls over low heat for 3–4 minutes. Increase to high heat and fry the balls until golden brown.
8. Serve warm.

PINEAPPLE PRAWNS 鳳梨蝦球

Serves 4

Pineapple with prawns was one of my favourite childhood dishes and is a dish that is popular in Chinese banquets. Chinese chefs usually garnish this dish with a little bit of colourful chocolate sprinkles. I'm not too sure why but they do add some colour and sweetness to the dish. If you're not a fan of chocolate sprinkles, you can use sesame instead.

370 g (13 oz) prawns, peeled and deveined

750 ml (24 fl oz / 3 cups) oil

280 g (10 oz) tinned pineapple, cut into 6 pieces, juice reserved

220 g cornflour, to coat prawns to deep-fry

Toasted black sesame seeds, to garnish

Marinade

1/2 egg

1 tsp salt

1 1/2 Tbsp cornflour

Sauce

2 1/2 Tbsp mayonnaise

1/2 tsp lemon juice

1 Tbsp castor sugar

Zest from 1 lemon

1. Rinse the prawns and pat dry with a clean kitchen towel.
2. Marinate the prawns in the ingredients for marinade for 30 minutes.
3. Heat the oil in a wok or deep saucepan over medium heat. Fry the prawns until golden. Drain the oil and set aside.
4. Using the same oil, fry the pineapple for 3–5 seconds. Drain the oil once more and set aside.
5. Place all the ingredients for sauce in a bowl and mix evenly.
6. Heat a clean wok over medium heat and add the sauce in. Cook for 10–15 seconds and add prawns and pineapples. Mix until the sauce coats the ingredients evenly.
7. Dish out. Garnish with black sesame seeds.
8. Serve.

STIR-FRIED CASHEW AND PRAWNS

腰果蝦仁

Serves 4

This dish is another one of my childhood favourite dishes. The sweet and crispy cashews go perfectly with the prawns. The sweet cashews make a delicious snack even without the prawns. You can double or triple the cashew recipe and make a lot of sweet cashews. These cashews can be stored in a clean and dry glass jar and kept in a dark and cool place for approximately two weeks.

85 g (3 oz) celery, cut into diamond shape

85 g (3 oz) red bell peppers, cut into diamond shape

2 Tbsp dried lily bulbs, soaked in hot water to soften

280 g (10 oz) prawns, peeled and deveined

150 g ($5^1/_3$ oz) sweet cashews

Salt, as needed

Sweet Cashews

200 g (7 oz) castor sugar

200 ml (7 fl oz) water

150 g ($5^1/_3$ oz) cashews

625 ml oil (20 fl oz / $2^1/_2$ cups) , to fry the cashews

Marinade

1 tsp cornflour

$^1/_2$ tsp salt

1 tsp rice wine

1 tsp cooking oil

1. Prepare the sweet cashews. Place castor sugar and water in a saucepan and bring to a boil. Add the cashews and cook over low heat for 20 minutes. Remove from the heat.
2. Place a sheet of parchment paper on a plate or tray. Transfer the sweet cashews to the plate.
3. Heat the oil in a wok or saucepan over low heat and fry the cashews until a light golden brown. Place the cashews on the parchment paper again.
4. Heat 1 Tbsp of oil in a wok over medium heat. Stir-fry the celery, bell peppers and lily bulb then add prawns.
5. Stir-fry for 20 seconds until the prawns turn red and are cooked. Add the cashews. Mix evenly. Adjust seasoning with salt.
6. Dish out and serve.

PRAWN FRIED RICE 蝦仁炒飯

Serves 3–4

Prawn fried rice is one of the most popular fried rice dishes in Chinese cooking. This recipe is really easy to make and only requires a handful of ingredients. It's really suitable for the beginner who wants to give Chinese cooking a go but also for more experienced cooks and chefs still love to make this dish.

- 15–20 prawns, peeled and deveined
- 4 large eggs, egg yolks and egg whites separated
- 300 g (11 oz) cold rice or leftover rice
- 70 g (2 1/2 oz) small carrot, diced
- 70 g (2 1/2 oz) frozen peas
- 2 Tbsp cooking oil
- 1/4 onion, peeled and finely chopped
- 2 Tbsp water
- 2 spring onions, green and white sections separated and finely chopped

Seasoning

- 1 salt
- 2 Tbsp light soy sauce
- 1/2 tsp sesame oil
- 1/2 tsp ground black pepper

1. Rinse the prawns in cold water and pat dry with a clean kitchen towel. Set aside.
2. Mix two egg yolks with cold rice evenly.
3. Cook the carrot in a pan of boiling water. When the carrot is almost done, add frozen peas and boil. Remove from the heat. Drain and place the carrot and peas in cold water immediately.
4. Heat 1 Tbsp of oil in a wok and stir-fry the onion until fragrant.
5. Add the prawns and stir-fry for 20 seconds. Add 2 Tbsp water and stir-fry for 10 seconds. Transfer the prawns to a plate or bowl. Set aside.
6. Beat the remaining egg whites and egg yolks together in a bowl.
7. Heat 1 Tbsp of oil in a wok over medium heat and stir-fry the green spring onions until fragrant.
8. Add the egg and stir-fry until the eggs are nearly cooked but still a little runny. Add rice and stir-fry to mix. Press down on any lumps to break them up.
9. Add the white spring onions, green peas and carrot and stir-fry for 1 more minute. Add the seasoning and mix well.
10. Dish out. Garnish as desired and serve.

Note: You can adjust the amount of seasoning to suit your personal taste.

GARLIC SAUCE AND VERMICELLI NOODLES WITH STEAMED SCALLOPS
蒜茸粉絲蒸扇貝

Serves 3

This scallop dish is absolutely delicious and all the ingredients combine perfectly to make it as flavoursome as it is. Sometimes I even think the vermicelli noodles taste better than the scallops and this dish is suitable for both banquets and special events. Why not treat your family and friends with this amazing scallop dish next time?

9 scallops, reserve 3 scallop shells
1 bunch of vermicelli noodles
2 Tbsp cooking oil
3 cloves garlic, peeled and finely chopped
2 chillies, seeded and finely chopped
2 spring onions, julienned

Seasoning
1 Tbsp rice wine
$^{1}/_{4}$ tsp ground white pepper
2 Tbsp light soy sauce
1 tsp demerara sugar
$^{1}/_{4}$ tsp sesame oil
$^{1}/_{2}$ tsp salt
1 Tbsp water

1. Rinse the scallops and remove tough membrane. Pat dry the scallops with a clean kitchen towel.
2. Soften the vermicelli noodles in warm water for 10–15 minutes. Boil a pot of water and blanch the vermicelli noodles for 8–10 seconds. Rinse under cold water immediately. Drain. Using a pair of scissors, cut the vermicelli noodles into shorter lengths.
3. Place the seasoning in a small bowl and mix evenly. Set aside for 20 minutes.
4. Heat 1 Tbsp oil in a wok over medium heat. Add garlic and chillies and turn off the heat immediately. Set aside for 5 minutes. Mix the garlic and chilli oil with seasoning.
5. Place a handful of vermicelli noodles on a scallop shell then top with 3 scallops.
6. Pour 1 Tbsp sauce on each portion of scallop. Steam the scallops for 6 minutes over high heat.
7. Garnish each portion of scallop with spring onion.
8. Heat 1 Tbsp oil and drizzle over the spring onion. Serve.

Note: You can adjust the amount of the soy sauce, salt, garlic and chilli to suit your personal taste preferences.

PRAWN AND PASSION FRUIT SALAD
百香果蝦仁沙拉

Make 8 portions

Summers in both Taiwan and China can be really hot and one of my favourite summer dishes for coping with the heat is this prawn and passion fruit salad. My grandfather made this very often during the summer and the presentation of the dish is very cute, so it's perfect for banquets and special events.

16 king prawns, peeled and deveined

8 passion fruits

1 Tbsp finely chopped coriander

2 cloves garlic, peeled and finely chopped

Seasoning

1 tsp chilli oil

1/4 tsp sesame oil

2 Tbsp light soy sauce

1/2 tsp salt

1 Tbsp fish sauce

1 Tbsp demerara sugar

2 Tbsp oil

1. Bring a pot of water to a boil over low heat. Blanch the prawns. Soak in cold water immediately after the prawns have cooked then drain the water.
2. Cut one-third of the passion fruit from the top. Using a spoon, dig out the passion fruit flesh and place in a mixing bowl. Repeat for all the passion fruits. Reserve the passion fruit skins for later.
3. Mix coriander, garlic and the seasoning with passion fruit and set aside for 20 minutes until all the seasoning are combined together.
4. Place the seasoned passion fruit back into the passion fruit skin. Top with two prawns.
5. Serve.

Note: You can adjust the amount of seasoning to suit your personal taste. For example, if you think 1 Tbsp of fish sauce is too strong for you then you could use just ½ Tbsp.

STIR-FRIED JUMBO PRAWNS IN SPICY SAUCE 干燒大蝦

Serves 4

We love this dish in our family but we usually only eat it on special occasions such as family gatherings, Chinese New Year dinner or even for making this cookbook. Red is a very lucky colour in Chinese culture. That's why we often cook this dish during Chinese New Year. The jumbo prawns in this dish are huge so I prepare one jumbo prawn per person (my husband usually eats about three!). Please be very careful when you fry the prawns as the oil can explode but this is why you try to get rid of as much water as possible after you've rinsed them.

4 jumbo prawns, rinsed and deveined

125 ml (4 fl oz / 1/2 cup) oil

1 Tbsp finely chopped ginger

3 cloves garlic, peeled and finely chopped

2 spring onions, finely chopped, reserve 1/2 Tbsp for garnish

1 chilli, seeded and finely chopped

Seasoning

1 1/2 Tbsp chilli bean sauce

3 Tbsp ketchup

1 Tbsp demerara sugar

1 tsp rice vinegar

180 ml (6 fl oz / 3/4 cup) vegetable or chicken stock (page 145)

Ground black pepper, as needed

1. Pat dry the prawns with a clean kitchen towel.
2. Heat the oil in a wok over medium heat. Pan-fry the prawns until red and transfer to a plate. Set aside.
3. With the remaining oil in the wok, stir-fry ginger, garlic, spring onions and chilli for 10–15 seconds.
4. Lower the heat, then add chilli bean sauce and stir-fry for 30 seconds.
5. Add the rest of the seasoning to wok and stir-fry for 1 minute.
6. Return the prawns to the wok and cook until the sauce reduces thickly.
7. Dish out the prawns and garnish with spring onions.
8. Serve.

STEAMED RAZOR CLAMS WITH BLACK BEANS AND CHILLI SAUCE
香辣豆豉蒸蟶子

Serves 3

I'm a little indifferent towards razor clams but my husband, my family and a huge number of Chinese and Taiwanese people love them. When you clean the razor clams, make sure you only keep the meat. This is a very quick and easy way to enjoy razor clams and I hope you will like it.

9–10 razor clams, rinsed

2 Tbsp oil

2 cloves garlic, peeled and finely chopped

1 chilli, seeded and finely chopped

1 spring onion, finely chopped

Seasoning

1 Tbsp oil

1 tsp Shaoxing rice wine

1/2 Tbsp light soy sauce

1 Tbsp black bean sauce

1. Pat dry razor clams with a clean kitchen towel.
2. Heat 1 Tbsp oil in a wok over medium heat. Fry the garlic and chilli but be very careful not to burn them so please cook at a low temperature.
3. Remove the garlic and chilli from heat. Mix with the seasoning in a bowl.
4. Place razor clams on a heatproof plate. Drizzle the seasoning over.
5. Steam for 5 minutes over high heat and once cooked, top the razor clams with spring onions.
6. Heat 1 Tbsp oil and drizzle over the cooked clams. Serve.

Note: Remove the stomach and the little sack that is full of sand. Never over cook razor clams as the meat will become really tough and it will be like trying to eat rubber boots.

SQUID STUFFED WITH SAVOURY STICKY RICE 糯米釀鮮魷

Makes 4

The way I like to cook the sticky rice for this dish is very similar to cooking risotto. You can adjust the amount of stock to cook the sticky rice. For example, if you like your rice al dente then you can use a little bit less water but if you want your rice quite soft then you just add a little more water and cook for longer.

4 medium squid tubes

4 bamboo skewers

Savoury Sticky Rice

110 g (4 oz) minced pork

4 dried shiitake mushrooms, rinsed

1 Tbsp dried prawns, rinsed

1 Tbsp oil

1 spring onion, finely chopped

140 g (5 oz) glutinous rice, rinsed

1 Tbsp dried shallots

Marinade

$^{1}/_{2}$ Tbsp light soy sauce

$^{1}/_{2}$ tsp dark soy sauce

$^{1}/_{2}$ Tbsp sugar

1 tsp rice wine

$^{1}/_{2}$ Tbsp oil

Seasoning

1 Tbsp light soy sauce

1 tsp demerara sugar

$^{1}/_{4}$ tsp ground white pepper

$^{1}/_{4}$ tsp blended sesame oil

375 ml (12 fl oz) hot water or stock (you can use vegetable or chicken stock) (page 145)

Seasoning for Squid Sauce

200 ml (7 fl oz) water

1 Tbsp dark soy sauce

$^{1}/_{2}$ Tbsp light soy sauce

1 tsp rice wine

1 spring onion, sliced into 3-cm ($1^{1}/_{4}$-in) lengths

2 slices ginger

1. Prepare the savoury sticky rice. Marinate the minced pork with the ingredients for the marinade for 30 minutes.
2. Soften the shiitake mushrooms and dried prawns in warm water for 15–20 minutes. Reserve the mushroom water. Chop the shiitake mushrooms finely.
3. Add all the ingredients for seasoning apart from hot water or stock into a bowl and mix well.
4. Heat 1 Tbsp of oil in a wok over medium heat. Stir-fry the spring onion for 5 seconds then add minced pork. Stir-fry until the minced pork is cooked.
5. Add the shiitake mushrooms and shrimps and stir-fry for 30 seconds.
6. Add the glutinous rice and stir-fry for another 20 seconds. Add the seasoning and stir continuously for 30 seconds.
7. Add hot water or stock, a little at a time. Lower to medium low heat. Repeat this procedure until the rice is soft or has reached desired texture.
8. Remove the rice from the heat. Transfer to a bowl or plate. Set aside to cool.

9. Once the rice is cooled, gently stuff rice into squid with a spoon. Using a skewer, sear and stabilize the opening of the squid to aid stuffing of the rice.
10. Heat a deep frying pan over medium heat and add the squid sauce. Bring to a boil then add the squid tubes. Cook for 3–4 minutes on each side.
11. Allow the squid to cool down before handling. Slice into desired number of pieces. Serve.

Note: You can make the sticky rice the night before and you only need to stuff the rice into the squid and finish cooking before serving.

SWEET AND SOUR FISH FILLET 糖醋魚柳

Serves 4

There are a few ways to make sweet and sour sauce but this ketchup-based version is a perfect match with deep-fried fish fillet. I used monkfish in this recipe but you can choose any other kind of "white flesh" fish for this dish. If you have a seafood or fish allergy, you may also replace the fish with chicken or pork. You can store this sweet and sour sauce in your fridge for 5–7 days and freeze it for 1 month. You can cook a big batch of the sauce, freeze it in portions and have the sauce ready whenever you want a sweet and sour dish.

450 g (1 lb) monkfish, diced
500 ml (16 fl oz / 2 cups) oil
¼ onion, peeled and diced
2 cloves garlic, peeled and sliced
½ green bell pepper, diced
½ orange bell pepper, diced
½ red bell pepper, diced
Salt, as needed

Marinade
1 tsp salt
1 tsp rice wine

Sweet and Sour Sauce
180 ml (6 fl oz / ¾ cup) water
90 ml (3 fl oz / ⅜ cup) ketchup
60 ml (2 fl oz / ¼ cup) rice vinegar
1 Tbsp black vinegar
85 g (3 oz) castor sugar
1 tsp salt
1½ tsp potato starch or cornflour
1 Tbsp water

Batter
1 Tbsp plain flour
1 egg white
½ Tbsp potato starch or cornflour
1 tsp cooking oil

1. Prepare the sweet and sour sauce. Place all the ingredients for sweet and sour sauce except potato starch or cornflour and water in a saucepan. Mix well.
2. Bring the sauce to a boil over low heat. Once boiled, lower the heat. Mix potato starch or cornflour with 1 Tbsp water. Stir potato slurry into the sauce.
3. Bring the sauce back to a boil then simmer over low heat for 8 minutes. Set aside.
4. Marinate the monkfish with the ingredients for marinade in a bowl for 30 minutes.
5. Add all the ingredients for the batter and mix until batter covers the fish evenly.
6. Heat the oil in a wok over medium heat and deep-fry the fish until golden. Remove from wok and drain the oil. Set aside.
7. Reheat the wok with a little oil. Stir-fry the onion and garlic until fragrant.
8. Add the bell peppers and stir-fry for 30 seconds. Adjust seasoning with salt.
9. Return the fried fish back to the wok. Mix well.
10. Add the sweet and sour sauce and mix well. Cook until the sauce reduces.
11. Dish out and serve.

Cumin
孜然
Dried Chilli
乾辣椒
Cumin
孜然
Dried Chilli
乾辣椒
Cumin
孜然
Dried Chilli
乾辣椒
Cumin
孜然
Dried Chilli
乾辣椒
Cumin
孜然
Dried Chilli
乾辣椒
Cumin
孜然
Dried Chilli
乾辣椒
Cumin
孜然
Dried Chilli
乾辣椒
Cumin
孜然
Dried Chilli
乾辣椒
Cumin
孜然
Dried Chilli
乾辣椒
Cumin
孜然
Dried Chilli
乾辣椒
Cumin
孜然
Dried Chilli
乾辣椒
Cumin
孜然
Dried Chilli
乾辣椒
Cumin
孜然

VEGETABLES

CHINESE CABBAGE AND CHIVE FLOWER SALAD 涼拌白菜心

Serves 5

The key to making this dish really delicious is to julienne the ingredients really finely so the ingredients can be seasoned quicker. Traditionally there are no chive flowers in this recipe but I add them as I personally think they make this salad look prettier. The chive flower is completely optional though so it's perfectly fine if you can't find them. When I was working as a chef, I always loved using flowers to garnish my salads because I've always feel felt that they can brighten the consumer's mood. It makes them feel special so I like to garnish my food with edible flowers.

500 ml (16 fl oz / 2 cups) cooking oil

55 g (2 oz) skinned peanuts

6 chive flowers, rinsed

375 g (13 1/5 oz) Chinese cabbage leaves, julienned

3 Asian dried tofu, julienned

1 chilli, julienned

A handful of coriander, roughly chopped

Seasoning

1 tsp blended sesame oil

1 tsp castor sugar

1 tsp Tbsp salt

1 Tbsp rice vinegar

1/2 Tbsp light soy sauce

1. Add the oil in a wok, then add peanuts. Fry the peanuts with cold oil rather than heating the oil first. This method will make the peanuts taste better and crunchier once fried. Fry the peanuts over medium heat.
2. Tear the chive flowers into small pieces with your hands.
3. Mix the seasoning and the rest of the ingredients together.
4. Place on a serving plate. Serve.

STIR-FRIED GARLIC SPROUTS WITH BEAN CURD 蒜苔炒豆干

Serves 3

This dish is a very common and popular dish in Chinese cooking. You can also add julienned beef or pork in this dish if you would like to have some meat.

Cooking oil, as needed

2 cloves garlic, peeled and finely chopped

1 chilli, seeded and julienned

140 g (5 oz) Asian dried tofu, thinly sliced

55 g (2 oz) wood ear, soaked in hot water to soften then julienned. The weight here is the weight of the wood ear after it has been softened.

2 Tbsp water

140 g (5 oz) garlic sprouts, sliced into 3-cm ($1^1/_4$-in) lengths

Seasoning

2 Tbsp light soy sauce

$^1/_2$ tsp salt

1 Tbsp demerara sugar

$^1/_4$ tsp ground black pepper

1. Heat the oil in a wok over medium heat. Stir-fry the garlic and chilli for 10 seconds.
2. Add the dried tofu, wood ear and 2 Tbsp water, then stir-fry for 1 minute.
3. Add the garlic sprouts to the wok and stir-fry for 30 seconds.
4. Add the seasoning and stir-fry for 30 seconds.
5. Dish out and serve.

LOTUS ROOT SALAD 涼拌蓮藕

Serves 2

This dish is ideally served ice cold but if you prefer to serve immediately after it has been prepared that's also fine. This is a great dish for hot weather because the lotus root is cold and crunchy and complements the sweet and sour sauce really well. The dish also helps people to regain their appetite during the hot weather. Lotus root has lots of healthy benefits and is very rich in nutrients. Some of the benefits include improving digestion, reducing cholesterol, lowering blood pressure and preventing various kinds of cancer. Even though I'm not medically trained and can't verify if these claims are true, I do believe having a variety of vegetables in your daily diet can only bring about benefits. Pickled cordia is an optional ingredient so you can still make this dish if you can't find this ingredient locally.

200 g (7 oz) lotus root

10–12 pickled cordia (optional)

1 chilli, seeded and julienned

1 celery stalk, you can use Chinese celery or western celery

1 spring onion, finely chopped

Sauce

2 Tbsp rice vinegar

2 Tbsp castor sugar

1 Tbsp water

1 tsp salt

1. Mix all the ingredients for the sauce in a bowl. Set aside.
2. Wash the lotus root thoroughly to remove any impurities. Peel the lotus root and thinly slice it.
3. Blanch lotus root in boiling water for a few minutes. Place lotus root in iced water to cool. Drain.
4. Mix the sauce and all the ingredients together in a bowl.
5. Place in a refrigerator to chill for a few hours before serving.
6. Serve chilled.

CUCUMBER STUFFED WITH STEAMED TARO MASH 芋泥蒸黄瓜

Make 8–10 portions

This is a vegetarian/vegan version of stuffed cucumber. Traditionally this dish is stuffed with minced pork but you can eat it without. If you do go for the version with the minced pork, I would recommend you put a single teaspoon of finely chopped ginger in the mince. If you have sensitive skin, you may want to wear gloves when you peel or cut taro root as it can cause skin irritation.

125 g (5 oz) taro, peeled and grated

55 g (2 oz) carrot, finely chopped

2 dried shiitake mushrooms, finely chopped

1 large cucumber, peeled and sliced into 4-cm (1½-in) thick pieces

A pinch of salt

Seasoning

1 tsp salt

½ Tbsp light soy sauce

¼ tsp blended sesame oil

½ Tbsp cornflour

½ Tbsp oil

½ Tbsp demerara sugar

1. Steam the taro for 20 minutes over high heat. Set aside to cool then mash coarsely.
2. Mix the carrot, shiitake mushrooms, mashed taro and the seasoning together in a large bowl.
3. Using a melon baller, dig a hole in each piece of cucumber. Do not dig all the way through.
4. Sprinkle a pinch of salt on the cucumber. Roll the minced mixture into small balls and place in the hollowed section of the cucumber.
5. Place the stuffed cucumber and mashed taro on a heatproof plate and steam for 8–10 minutes over medium heat.
6. Serve warm.

CHINESE EGGPLANTS IN GARLIC AND CHILLI SAUCE 凉拌茄子

Serves 3

Apart from the fragrant eggplant with fish sauce recipe, this is the other eggplant recipe that I really love and I ate this dish quite often when I grew up as my family. My grandfather sometimes added chilli oil and Sichuan pepper oil to give this dish a big of a "kick" as he was an old traditional Sichuanese person who loves spicy, mouth numbing food.

3 eggplants, sliced into 4-cm (1½-in) long sections

Water for boiling

1½ Tbsp rice vinegar

1 tsp salt

2 Tbsp cooking oil

Sauce

3 cloves garlic, peeled and finely chopped

1 spring onion, finely chopped

1 chilli, seeded and finely chopped

2 Tbsp finely chopped coriander

2 Tbsp light soy sauce

1 tsp black vinegar

½ tsp blended sesame oil

2 Tbsp oil

1 Tbsp demerara sugar

1. Cut the eggplant sections into quarters. Soak the eggplants in water.
2. Bring the water to a boil in a stockpot. Add the rice vinegar and salt. Cook the eggplants.
3. Heat the oil in a wok over medium heat. Add the garlic and turn off heat immediately.
4. Add all the ingredients for the sauce and fried garlic together in a bowl. Mix well and set aside for at least 30 minutes.
5. Add the eggplants and close the lid immediately. Cook for 1 minute and cool down in iced water immediately after. Drain the water and set aside.
6. Place the eggplants on a serving plate and pour the sauce over.
7. Garnish as desired. Serve.

DEEP-FRIED TOFU COATED WITH BLACK SESAME 黑芝麻炸豆腐

Serves 4

Deep-fried tofu is one of my favourite Chinese vegan tofu dishes. You can use black sesame, white sesame, pistachio, walnuts and peanuts for coating the tofu as long as you chop the pistachio or walnuts really finely, which will make coating the tofu easier.

800 g (1 $^{3}/_{4}$ lb) firm tofu

2 small eggs, beaten

4 Tbsp plain flour

750 ml (24 fl oz / 3 cups) cooking oil

Pistachio Breadcrumbs

45 g (1 $^{1}/_{2}$ oz) pistachios, finely chopped

$^{1}/_{4}$ tsp salt

4 Tbsp panko breadcrumbs

Black Sesame Breadcrumbs

1 $^{1}/_{2}$ Tbsp black sesame seeds

$^{1}/_{4}$ tsp salt

4 Tbsp panko breadcrumbs

1. Cut the tofu into 1 x 6-cm ($^{1}/_{2}$ x 1 $^{3}/_{5}$-in) rectangles.
2. Mix all the ingredients for the pistachio breadcrumbs together in a shallow plate.
3. Mix all the ingredients for the black sesame bread crumbs together in another shallow plate.
4. Place the flour in a bowl. Coat the tofu with flour first then egg and pistachio breadcrumbs or black sesame breadcrumbs. Repeat this procedure until all the tofu are coated.
5. Heat the oil in a saucepan or wok to 180°C (350°F). Alternatively, you can also place a few breadcrumbs in the oil and check if the oil bubbles.
6. Deep-fry the tofu until lightly golden brown.
7. Serve with ketchup or sweet chilli sauce as preferred.

CUCUMBER AND WOOD EAR SALAD
涼拌黃瓜木耳

Serves 3

This dish is very popular during the summer and traditionally, cucumbers have been used as the main ingredient. I added the wood ear into this recipe because wood ears are delicious, high in nutrients and match the rest of the ingredients perfectly. I would highly recommend you make this dish at least 30 minutes before serving as the sauce and vegetables take some time to marinate.

45 g ($1^1/_2$ oz) wood ears (this weight is after the wood ear has soften in water.)

280 g (10 oz) cucumber, seeded and sliced into four 3-cm ($1^1/_4$-in) long sections

1 chilli, seeded and julienned

1 clove garlic, peeled and finely chopped

1–2 tsp white sesame seeds

Seasoning

2 Tbsp rice vinegar

$^1/_2$ tsp blended sesame oil

2 Tbsp castor sugar

1 tsp salt

1 tsp light soy sauce

1. Using both hands, tear the wood ears into small pieces.
2. Cook the wood ears in boiling water for 5 minutes. Drain and rinse in cold water. Drain.
3. Mix the seasoning together with the wood ear, cucumber, chilli and garlic. Set aside for 30 minutes.
4. Dish out. Garnish with white sesame seeds and serve.

KUNG PAO TOFU 宫保豆腐

Serves 4

This dish is a vegetarian version of *kung pao* chicken. It's so delicious even without chicken and is one of the very few vegetarian dishes I can get my husband to eat. When you cook this dish, use a wooden spoon to gently and slowly "push" the tofu in the wok rather than stir it. This is how you keep the tofu in shape without accidentally mashing it during the cooking process.

700 g ($1\frac{1}{2}$ lb) firm tofu, cut into 1.5–2-cm cubes

3 Tbsp plain flour

85 g (3 oz) skinned peanuts

625 ml (20 fl oz / $2\frac{1}{2}$ cups) cooking oil

5 dried chillies, halved

2 cloves garlic, peeled and chopped

1 tsp finely chopped ginger

180 g ($6\frac{1}{3}$ oz) edamame beans or broad beans

1 spring onion, sliced into 3-cm ($1\frac{1}{4}$-in) lengths

Seasoning

2 Tbsp light soy sauce

2 Tbsp water

1 Tbsp ketchup

$\frac{1}{2}$ tsp salt

1 Tbsp demerara sugar

1 tsp dark soy sauce

Sesame oil, as needed

1. Line a plate with a few sheets of kitchen towels to get rid of any excess water.
2. Coat the tofu with flour.
3. Add the peanuts and oil into a wok or saucepan. Deep-fry the peanuts until a light golden brown. Drain the oil and set aside once cooked.
4. Using the same oil, heat the wok to 180°C (350°F) and deep-fry the tofu until light golden. Drain the oil and set aside.
5. Heat 1 Tbsp oil and stir-fry the dried chillies for 20 seconds.
6. Stir-fry the garlic and ginger until fragrant.
7. Add the tofu, edamame beans or broad beans and all the ingredients from the seasoning apart from sesame oil. Cook until the sauce reduces down to half the amount. Using a wooden spoon, gently push the tofu around in the wok during the cooking process.
8. Add the spring onion and sesame oil and cook for another 30 seconds.
9. Dish out. Garnish as desired and serve with rice.

Note: You can also add some mushrooms in this recipe.

STIR-FRIED BITTER MELON WITH DRIED PRAWNS 虾米炒苦瓜

Serves 3

There are many ways to cook bitter melon but this is one of the easiest and quickest ways to prepare this dish. Bitter melon tastes bitter just like the name. Some people love the taste while others absolutely hate. The bitter melon I use is green bitter melon and they are quite small in size. The white bitter melon is of a different variety and is more common in the East. In Chinese culture, it's believed that eating bitter melon can help reduce your blood sugar and also help your liver and body to detox, but as always, it is best to eat all food in moderation.

2 small green bitter melons

2 Tbsp dried prawns, soaked in hot water to soften

Cooking oil, as needed

2 cloves garlic, finely chopped

1 chilli, seeded and finely chopped

1 Tbsp water

Seasoning

1 Tbsp light soy sauce

1/2 Tbsp demerara sugar

1/2 tsp salt

1/2 tsp rice wine

1. Cut bitter melons into half lengthwise. Using a small metal spoon, remove the seeds and cut into thin slices.
2. Drain the dried prawns and set aside.
3. Heat the oil in a wok over medium heat. Stir-fry the garlic and chilli until fragrant.
4. Add the dried prawns and stir-fry for 10 seconds.
5. Add the bitter melon and water. Stir-fry for a few minutes.
6. Add the seasoning and stir-fry for 1 minute.
7. Dish out. Garnish as desired and serve.

Liquorice Root 甘草
Nutmeg 肉荳蔻
Liquorice Root 甘草
Nutmeg 肉荳蔻
Liquorice Root 甘草
Nutmeg 肉荳蔻
Liquorice Root 甘草
Nutmeg 肉荳蔻
Liquorice Root 甘草
Nutmeg 肉荳蔻
Liquorice Root 甘草
Nutmeg 肉荳蔻
Liquorice Root 甘草
Nutmeg 肉荳蔻
Liquorice Root 甘草
Nutmeg 肉荳蔻
Liquorice Root 甘草
Nutmeg 肉荳蔻
Liquorice Root 甘草
Nutmeg 肉荳蔻
Liquorice Root 甘草
Nutmeg 肉荳蔻
Liquorice Root 甘草
Nutmeg 肉荳蔻
Liquorice Root 甘草

SOUPS

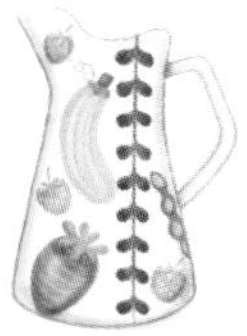

TOFU PARCEL SOUP 百寶袋湯

Serves 4

Tofu parcel soup is a dish that's not only delicious but also very suitable for serving in banquets. The tofu parcels look like money sacks so this dish can also be served during the Chinese New Year period.

300 g (11 oz) minced pork or beef

1 spring onion, finely chopped

2 dried shiitake mushrooms, softened in water and finely chopped

12 fried soybean curd

12 spring onions, green sections only, blanched

Seasoning

1 Tbsp light soy sauce

1/2 Tbsp demerara sugar

1/2 tsp ground white pepper

1/2 tsp salt

1/4 tsp blended sesame oil

Soup

1.25 litres (40 fl oz / 5 cups) chicken stock or vegetable stock (page 145)

2 celery stalks, diced

1 carrot, peeled and diced

Salt, as needed

Ground white pepper, as needed

1. Mix the seasoning with minced pork or beef, spring onion and shiitake mushrooms.
2. Fill the soybean curd with minced mixture. Seal the opening with the green section of the spring onion. Tie into a knot. Repeat for all the soy bean curd.
3. Prepare the soup. Place the chicken or vegetable stock, celery and carrot in a saucepan. Bring to a boil.
4. Add the tofu parcels and bring it to a boil, then simmer over low heat for 15 minutes.
5. Season with salt and ground white pepper.
6. Dish out. Serve with rice.

Note: The soy bean curd used in this recipe is the same one that is used for the Japanese *inari* sushi, *ajitsuke inari*.

BEEF SHANK, POTATO AND TOMATO SOUP 牛肉羅宋湯

Serves 5–6

This is one of the soups I really liked when I was young. This is also one of the best dishes my father cooked when I grew up and he added a lot of other vegetables in his soup. If you like, you can add green peas and cabbage as well. Feel free to adjust the seasoning to suit your personal preference.

700 g (1½ lb) beef shin or flank, diced or sliced

3 slices ginger

1 spring onion

1 banana shallot or 3 cloves shallots

1.25 litres (40 fl oz / 5 cups) beef stock

450 g (1 lb) tomato, cut into chunks

280 g (10 oz) carrots, peeled and cut into chunks

3 potatoes, peeled and cut into large chunks

Chopped coriander, as needed

Seasoning

1 tsp salt

3 Tbsp light soy sauce

2 Tbsp rice wine

1. Blanch the beef in boiling water for a few minutes. Drain and place in cold water.
2. Place the seasoning, ginger, spring onion, banana shallot or shallots, beef stock and beef in a stockpot. Bring to a boil, then simmer over low heat for 1 hour.
3. Add the tomato and simmer for another hour.
4. Add the carrots and potatoes and cook until the carrot and potatoes are soft.
5. Garnish with the chopped coriander. Serve.

APPLE RIBS SOUP 蘋果排骨湯

Serves 4

Many Chinese people believe this soup is very good for your body. A lot of ladies like to drink this soup to get healthier and shinier skin. People also believe this soup can help you to improve your memory. Of course these sayings are just for recommendation but I believe the old English saying, "an apple a day keeps the doctor away" still holds.

450 g (1 lb) pork ribs, cut into 3–4-cm (1¼–1½-in) pieces

Water to cover the ribs

6 dried jujubes (Chinese red dates), rinsed in cold water

2 red apples, peeled, cored and diced

Salt, as needed

Ground white pepper, as needed

1. Blanch the ribs then rinse in cold water.
2. Place the ribs and water into a stockpot. Bring to a boil then add jujubes. Simmer over low heat for 30 minutes.
3. Add the apples and simmer for 1 hour.
4. Season with salt and ground white pepper.
5. Serve.

LOTUS ROOT RIBS SOUP 蓮藕排骨湯

Serves 4

My grandmother is originally from Guangzhou, China and people from that part of China really like soup. They believe soup is one of the best things for the human body so my grandmother cooks all kinds of seasonal soups throughout the year. I've loved this soup ever since she prepared it for me for the first time. The dried squid helps to enhance the flavour of the soup but you can cook the soup without it if you can't get hold of this ingredient.

2 lotus roots

1 10 g (1/3 oz) small dried squid

Cooking oil, as needed

3 gloves garlic, peeled

700 g (1 1/2 lb) pork ribs, cut into 3–4-cm (1 1/4–1 1/2-in) long sections

2 spring onions, sliced

2 litres (64 fl oz / 8 cups) water

Seasoning

1 Tbsp rice wine

Salt, as needed

Ground white pepper, as needed

1. Wash the lotus roots thoroughly to remove dirt and any impurities. Slice lotus roots thickly.
2. Soften the dried squid in warm water then drain and slice.
3. Heat some oil in a wok over medium heat. Fry the squid. Remove from the wok. Set aside.
4. Blanch the pork ribs in a pot of boiling water. Drain. Rinse in cold water and drain.
5. Place all the ingredients in a stockpot and bring to a boil. Simmer over low heat for 1 hour.
6. Add the seasoning and simmer for another 20 minutes.
7. Garnish as desired. Serve.

HOT AND SOUR SOUP 酸辣湯

Serves 4–5

This is one of the most popular soups in Chinese food. I love to have this soup with my dumplings. You can adjust the amount of the seasoning to suit your personal preference. I add the vinegar at the end so that people can still taste the tartness of the vinegar.

1 Tbsp cooking oil

70 g (2 1/2 oz) carrot, julienned

140 g (5 oz) Chinese leaves, thinly sliced

4 dried shiitake mushrooms, soaked in hot water to soften

70 g (2 1/2 oz) wood ear, julienned

100 g (3 1/2 oz) bamboo shoots, julienned

435 ml (14 fl oz) chicken stock (page 145)

280 g (10 oz) firm tofu, julienned

1 large egg, beaten

A handful of chopped coriander leaves

Sliced red chillies

Blended sesame oil, as needed

Seasoning

2 Tbsp light soy sauce

1 tsp salt

Potato starch water (1 Tbsp potato starch mixed with 1 Tbsp water)

1/2 tsp ground white pepper

1 Tbsp rice vinegar

2 Tbsp black vinegar

1. Heat 1 Tbsp oil in a wok over medium heat. Stir-fry the carrot and Chinese leaves for 30 seconds.
2. Squeeze the excess water from the shiitake mushrooms and reserve the soaking liquid. Slice the mushrooms thinly.
3. Add the wood ear, bamboo shoots and shiitake mushrooms and stir-fry for 30 seconds.
4. Add the chicken stock and the liquid from soaking the shiitake mushrooms. Bring to a boil, then simmer over low heat for 5–8 minutes.
5. Add the light soy sauce and salt and cook for 3–4 minutes.
6. Stir in potato starch water and bring to a boil.
7. Add the tofu and egg and gently stir for 3–4 times.
8. Add the ground white pepper, rice vinegar, black vinegar and turn off the heat.
9. Garnish as desired and add a few drops of sesame oil.
10. Serve warm.

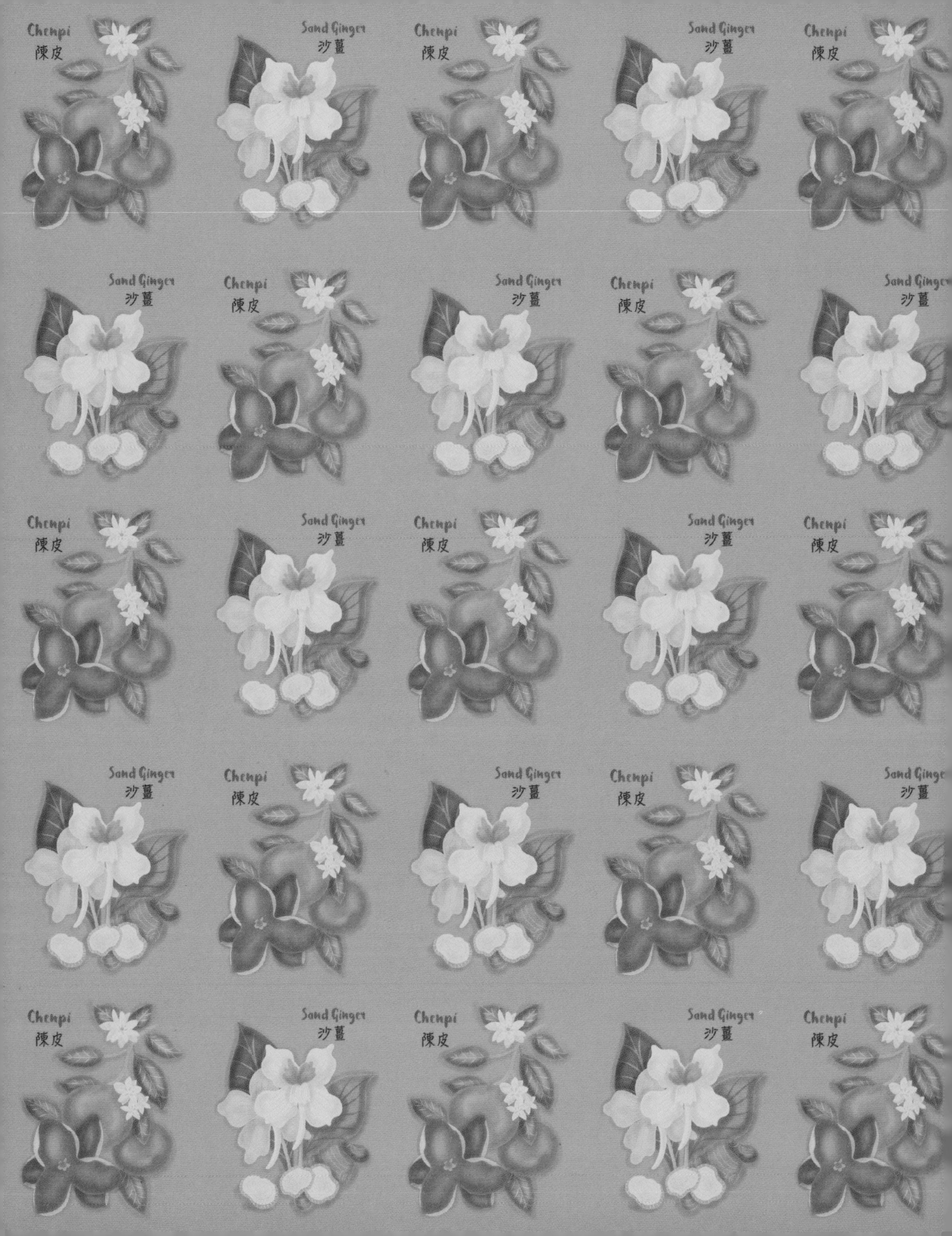
Chenpi
陳皮
Sand Ginger
沙薑

DESSERTS

STEAMED LOTUS ROOT STUFFED WITH SWEET STICKY RICE 蜜汁蒸米藕

Serves 3

This is one of my favourite Chinese desserts. The lotus root and glutinous rice make a perfect combination and the lotus root also gives the glutinous rice a refreshing fragrance. The osmanthus flower in this recipe is completely optional so you can do without it if you cannot get hold of the ingredient.

2 lotus roots

100 g (3½ oz) short-grained glutinous rice, soaked for 1 hour

2–3 cocktail skewers

Water to cover the lotus root

5–6 dried jujubes (Chinese red dates)

70 g (2½ oz) rock sugar

1 Tbsp dried osmanthus flower (optional)

70 g (2½ oz) demerara sugar

2 Tbsp honey

1. Wash the lotus root thoroughly to remove dirt and any impurities. Peel the lotus root. Cut one-quarter of the lotus root off. Reserve as a lid.
2. Stuff the glutinous rice into the holes of the lotus root. Using a pair of chopsticks, gently push the rice to fill in the gaps.
3. Use 2–3 cocktail skewers to fasten the lid to the lotus root.
4. Bring a pot of water to a boil in a large pot. Add jujubes, rock sugar and osmanthus flower. Allow ingredients to boil then lower stuffed lotus root into the water. Simmer for 1.5 hours.
5. Reserve 250 ml (8 fl oz / 1 cup) of the boiling liquid. Add sugar and honey. Boil the mixture and simmer until the sauce has reduced down to half the original amount. Set aside. Use this as a sauce for the lotus root.
6. Slice the stuffed lotus root thinly and place on a serving plate. Drizzle honey syrup on top of the lotus root.
7. Garnish as desired. Serve.

EIGHT TREASURE RICE PUDDING 八寶飯

Serves 4

Eight treasure rice pudding is a traditional Chinese New Year pudding. This pudding is made with eight different kinds of dried fruits, raisins and sweets. You can choose ingredients that are easily available for you. It's traditional to have eight different toppings for this dessert but you can use as many toppings as you want to. I used five different kinds of toppings today as eight toppings would be too much for this small serving. The number eight is a special number for the Chinese as it sounds like another Chinese word "發", which means to prosper. That is why eight is often considered an auspicious number.

680 g round glutinous rice

1 Tbsp sunflower oil + more as needed

Salt, as needed

A handful of sugar glazed cherries, halved

A handful of black raisins

A handful of yellow raisins

A handful of sugar lotus seeds

1 dried apricot

100 g (3½ oz) red bean paste

Seasoning

1 Tbsp honey

Sugar Syrup

125 ml (4 fl oz / ½ cup) water

A few drops of rose water (optional)

2 Tbsp potato starch water (½ tsp potato starch with 1 Tbsp water and mix evenly)

1. Soak the glutinous rice in cold water for at least 1 hour. Cook in a rice cooker or steamer. Mix the cooked rice with sunflower oil and salt while it is still hot.
2. Brush some oil on a medium bowl. Place the dried apricot in the centre. Line sugar glazed cherries around the apricot, then do the same for the black and yellow raisins.
3. Place half the amount of cooked glutinous rice in the bowl and press down a little. Place 100 g (3½ oz) red bean paste in the centre.
4. Using a little glutinous rice, cover the red bean paste and place the sugar lotus seeds and sugar glazed cherries around the bowl.
5. Place the remaining glutinous rice in the bowl and press down to compact rice. Steam for 30 minutes. Brush the honey over the fruits and rice.
6. Prepare sugar syrup. Bring water and rose water to a boil in a small pot. Stir in potato starch water to thicken the syrup.
7. Turn the rice pudding over on a serving plate and brush sugar syrup on top.
8. Serve.

STEWED PEARS WITH JUJUBE AND SYRUP 紅棗桂花燉雪梨

Serves 4

When I was young, my mother and grandmother would always take me out to eat this dish if I had a sore throat. In Chinese cooking, people believe that this dessert is really good for your throat and lungs. So if you have a sore throat, a nasty flu or cold or maybe you've lost your voice, you know which dessert to go for next time.

4 Chinese pears

Juice from 2 lemons

750 ml (24 fl oz / 3 cups) water

200 g (7 oz) rock sugar

2 Tbsp honey

$^{1}/_{2}$ tsp salt

1 Tbsp dried osmanthus flowers (optional)

12 dried jujubes (Chinese red dates)

1. Peel the pears and remove the cores. Soak in water with half the amount of lemon juice to prevent pears from oxidising.
2. Place the pears, water, rock sugar, honey, salt and the remaining amount of lemon juice in a saucepan. The pears have to be submerged in the water.
3. Bring to a boil, then simmer over low heat for 10 minutes.
4. Add the osmanthus flowers and jujubes and simmer for another 20 minutes.
5. Serve.

RASPBERRY SNOWFLAKE CAKE
覆盆梅雪花糕

Serves 4

雪花糕 is the Chinese name of this dessert and "雪花" means snowflake. This dish is easily translated as snowflake cake. Traditionally, this dessert is not made of raspberry but they are easily available in the UK. I love the taste of raspberries and think they work really well with this dish. If you do not like raspberries, you could use mangoes as well.

55 g (2 oz) raspberries

450 ml (15 1/5 fl oz) water

200 g (7 oz) castor sugar

200 ml (7 fl oz) milk

60 ml (2 fl oz / 1/4 cup) double cream

5 gelatin leaves, softened in cold water

125 g (4 1/2 oz) potato starch

100 ml (3 1/2 fl oz) water

3 Tbsp desiccated coconut

1. Cook the raspberries, water and castor sugar in a small saucepan and bring to a boil. Keep whisking while cooking to help the sugar and raspberries dissolve.
2. Add the milk and double cream and bring back to a boil. Once it has started boiling, turn off the heat and set aside for 10 minutes.
3. Add the gelatin and continue whisking to mix well.
4. Mix the potato starch and water well and add to saucepan. Remove the mixture from heat.
5. Line a sheet of parchment paper in a baking tray. Pour the mixture into this tray and set aside in a refrigerator for a few hours to chill and set.
6. Slice the chilled snowflake cake as desired. Coat with the desiccated coconut and serve.

STEAMED RICE CAKE WITH SWEET RED BEAN FILLING 愛窩窩

Make 8–9 portions

This dessert is a classic Chinese dessert that comes with a long history. The red bean filling takes a long time to make but I highly recommend you make a big batch of it and store in a clean and dry container. Once it's completely cooled, place the filling in your refrigerator. They can be stored for up to one month.

450 g (1 lb) cooked round glutinous rice

55 g (2 oz) potato starch

Candied Jujubes

180 ml (6 fl oz / ¾ cup) water

100 g (3½ oz) castor sugar

8 dried jujubes (Chinese red dates), soaked in warm water for 1 hour

Red Bean Filling

200 g (7 oz) red beans, soaked in 500 ml (16 fl oz / 2 cups) water overnight

1 litre (32 fl oz / 4 cups) water

85 g (3 oz) castor sugar

1 tsp salt

1 Tbsp cooking oil

45 g (1½ oz) toasted walnuts, roughly chopped

1. Prepare the candied jujubes. Bring water and castor sugar to a boil in a pot, then simmer over low heat for 10 minutes.
2. Add the jujubes and simmer for 30 minutes. Add more water if there is barely any water left.
3. Prepare the red bean filling. Bring red beans and water to a boil in a large pot, then simmer over low heat for 2 hours. Cook until the water has nearly dried out and the red beans are soft.
4. Using a hand masher, mash the red beans until they form a paste. Cook the red beans over low heat. Slowly stir in castor sugar and salt. Cook for a few more minutes. Transfer to a heatproof container or bowl. Slowly stir in oil. Set aside to cool.
5. Add the walnuts and mix well. Roll filling into small bowls and place in the refrigerator for 30–40 minutes to chill.
6. Preheat the oven to 180°C (350°F). Place the potato starch in a baking tray.
7. Place the potato starch in the oven and turn the oven off immediately. Leave the potato starch in the oven for 5–6 minutes.
8. Pound the glutinous rice with a rolling pin when the rice is still hot.
9. Separate the rice into 8 balls and gently flatten the rice balls. Place red bean filling in the centre and wrap with the rice.
10. Gently press the rice ball down and coat with cooked potato starch and place a candied jujube on top. Serve.

Note: Soak red beans for at least 6 hours or overnight as recommended.

GINGER MILK CURD WITH PLUM COMPOTE
薑汁燉奶佐燉梅子

Make 3 small bowls

This is one of my favourite Chinese desserts and one with which you can easily get hold of all the ingredients from your local supermarket. Traditionally, people don't serve this dessert with plum compote but I made plum compote because I find that the ginger flavour goes really nicely with the plum compote. Hopefully, you will enjoy this dessert as much as I do.

Plum Compote

180 ml (6 fl oz / $^{3}/_{4}$ cup) water

85 g (3 oz) castor sugar

280 g (10 oz) plums, stoned

1 cinnamon stick

1 star anise

Ginger Milk Curd

1 Tbsp ginger juice

4 egg whites

375 ml (12 fl oz) whole milk

90 g ($3^{1}/_{5}$ oz) castor sugar

1. Prepare the plum compote. Bring water to a boil in a saucepan, then add sugar and mix well. Cook for 1 minute over medium heat.
2. Add the plums and spices and simmer over low heat for 10 minutes.
3. Remove plums and reduce the sauce until the sauce is thick like syrup.
4. Prepare the ginger milk curd. Mix ginger juice with egg whites together in a bowl.
5. Warm the milk and sugar over low heat in a pot until near boiling point. Stir into the ginger juice mixture, a little at a time. Mix well.
6. Pass the mixture though a fine sift. Repeat thrice.
7. Steam the three heatproof bowls over high heat for a few minutes.
8. Pour the mixture into the bowls and cover with a sheet of tin foil on top. Steam for 5 minutes over high heat.
9. Continue steaming for 10 minutes over low heat.
10. Remove from the heat. Serve.

Note: To get ginger juice from fresh ginger, grate ginger very finely and wrap the ginger in a clean muslin cloth. Squeeze the ginger in the muslin cloth to a bowl and you will see the juice comes out very easily.

Cover the ginger milk curd with tin foil just in case the water spills over and drips into the milk curd during the cooking/steaming process.

BUTTERNUT SQUASH AND COCONUT JELLY WITH OSMANTHUS
桂花椰奶南瓜糕

Serves 7

Traditionally, people use pumpkin instead of butternut squash for this dessert but apart from October (Halloween), it seems to be really hard to get hold of pumpkin in the UK. The pumpkin in the UK tastes very different to Eastern pumpkin (less sweet and harder texture) so I replaced the pumpkin with butternut squash.

400 g (14 1/3 oz) butternut squash, peeled and seeded

15 g (1/2 oz) rock sugar

60 ml (2 fl oz / 1/4 cup) condensed milk

400 ml (13 1/2 fl oz) coconut milk

1 Tbsp dried osmanthus flowers, reserve a little for garnish

5 gelatin leaves, softened in cold water

1. Cut the butternut squash into small pieces.
2. Place all the ingredients apart from the gelatin in a saucepan and bring to a boil.
3. Simmer over low heat for 30 minutes until the butternut squash is soft. Turn off the heat and set aside to cool down for 10 minutes.
4. Using a smoothie machine or food processor, process the butternut squash mixture.
5. Stir the softened gelatin into butternut squash mixture. Pour mixture into jelly moulds.
6. Place the jelly moulds in the refrigerator for 1 hour to chill and set.
7. Garnish with osmanthus flower. Serve chilled.

HIBISCUS JELLY WITH FRUITS
洛神花果凍

Make 6–8

This is one of my favourite summer desserts. It's cold, sweet and sour and also full of Vitamin C, which is good for the skin. In Chinese cooking, people believe that the hibiscus flower is good for losing weight and also good for your skin. It also has the ability to help you relax, detox your body so people really like to use hibiscus to make desserts, cold drinks and tea.

500 ml (16 fl oz / 2 cups) water
10–12 dried hibiscus flowers
Juice from ½ lemon
70 g (2½ oz) rock sugar
4 gelatin leaves
½ dragon fruit, diced
1 kiwi, peeled and diced
½ strawberry, diced

1. Bring water, hibiscus flowers, lemon juice and rock sugar to a boil in a pot.
2. Simmer over low heat for 20 minutes. Remove hibiscus flowers.
3. Soften the gelatin in cold water then stir into hibiscus syrup.
4. Place the diced fruits in the serving glasses. Pour hibiscus jelly into the glasses.
5. Place in the refrigerator for a few hours to chill and set.
6. Serve chilled.

OSMANTHUS AND GOJI BERRIES JELLY
枸紀桂花糕

Makes 4 jellies

Chinese people like to use osmanthus flowers to make desserts because these flowers have a really lovely fragrance. It's a bit like how Western people use rose or rose water to make desserts. This dessert is very light and full of osmanthus flower fragrance.

500 ml (16 fl oz / 2 cups) water
100 g (3½ oz) castor sugar
2 Tbsp wolfberries (goji berries)
1 Tbsp dried osmanthus flowers
5 gelatin leaves

1. Place water and castor sugar in a saucepan and bring to a boil.
2. Add the goji berries and osmanthus flowers and simmer over low heat for 10 minutes.
3. Turn off the heat. Set aside to cool for 10 minutes.
4. Soften the gelatin in cold water and stir into saucepan.
5. Pour the mixture into jelly moulds.
6. Place the jelly in the refrigerator for a few hours to chill and set.
7. Serve cold.

ROSE AND ANNIN TOFU WITH FRUITS 玫瑰杏仁豆腐

Serves 3–4

Traditionally, this dessert is served with fruit and plain syrup but I quite like using flowers in my dishes so I tried something a bit different with this recipe. Instead of using plain syrup, I used rose syrup. But if you're not a big fan of rose, you can choose to use plain syrup instead. You can adjust the amount of sugar and ground apricot kernels to suit your personal taste. You can also make the annin tofu ahead so you just need to plate it before serving.

6–8 strawberries, remove the leaves and cut into halves or quarters

2 kiwis, peeled and diced

Annin Tofu

30 g (1 oz) ground apricot kernels

500 ml (16 fl oz / 2 cups) whole milk

90 ml (3 fl oz / 3/8 cup) water

70 g (2 1/2 oz) castor sugar

4–5 gelatin leaves

Rose Syrup

12 dried pink roses

375 ml (12 fl oz) water

70 g (2 1/2 oz) castor sugar

1/2 tsp rose water

1. Prepare the annin tofu. Place all the ingredients apart from the gelatin into a saucepan. Bring to a boil, then simmer over low heat for 20 minutes. Set aside to cool down for 10–15 minutes.
2. Soften the gelatin in cold water and stir into saucepan.
3. Pass the mixture through a fine sift a few times.
4. Line a sheet of parchment paper in a baking tray and pour the mixture in. Place in the refrigerator for a few hours to chill and set.
5. Prepare the rose syrup. Place all the ingredients for the rose syrup together in a saucepan. Bring to a boil, then simmer over low heat for 20 minutes.
6. Remove from the heat. Set aside to cool.
7. Remove the chilled annin tofu from the refrigerator. Gently remove from the baking tray. Cut into small cubes as desired.
8. Serve with rose syrup and fruit.

BASIC STOCKS

I have provided recipes for some basic stocks which you can use whenever a recipe calls for stock. The stocks will keep refrigerated for up to a week and in the freezer for up to a month. You can also put them in small containers for freezing and thaw only what you need. Although home-made stock does taste better, you can always substitute with stock cubes or ready-made stock from the supermarket if you do not have the time to make the stock from scratch.

VEGETABLE STOCK

Makes about 2 litres (64 fl oz / 8 cups)

- 200 g (7 oz) onions, peeled and roughly chopped
- 200 g (7 oz) carrots, peeled and roughly chopped
- 120 g (4$^1/_3$ oz) leeks, peeled and roughly chopped
- 120 g (4$^1/_3$ oz) celery, peeled and roughly chopped
- 2.5 litres (80 fl oz / 10 cups) water

1. Place all the ingredients into a large stockpot. Bring to a boil, then simmer over low heat for 1$^1/_2$ hours. Strain and use as needed.

CHICKEN STOCK

Makes about 2 litres (64 fl oz / 8 cups)

- 200 g (7 oz) chicken bones
- 150 g (5$^1/_3$ oz) onion, peeled and roughly chopped
- 120 g (4$^1/_3$ oz) carrot, peeled and roughly chopped
- 90 g (3$^1/_4$ oz) celery, roughly chopped
- 2.5 litres (80 fl oz / 10 cups) water

1. Blanch the chicken bones and rinse under cold water.
2. Place all the ingredients into a large stockpot. Bring to a boil, then simmer over low heat for 2 hours. Skim off any scum that rises to the surface from time to time. Strain and use as needed.

PORK STOCK

Makes about 1.5 litres (48 fl oz / 6 cups)

- 300 g (11 oz) pork bones
- 150 g (5$^1/_3$ oz) onion, peeled and roughly chopped
- 120 g (4$^1/_3$ oz) carrot, peeled and roughly chopped
- 90 g (3$^1/_4$ oz) celery, roughly chopped
- 2.5 litres (80 fl oz / 10 cups) water

1. Blanch the pork bones and rinse under cold water.
2. Place all the ingredients into a large stockpot. Bring to a boil, the simmer over low heat for 3–4 hours. Skim off any scum that rises to the surface from time to time. Strain and use as needed.

GLOSSARY
Flour

FRESH AND DRIED INGREDIENTS

Bamboo shoot

Bamboo shoot is eaten as a vegetable and it is very popular in Taiwan where it is used in many dishes, from soups and stews to salads and stir-fries. The young shoots of the bamboo plant are harvested in the spring and summer, but sometimes, depending on how warm the seasons are, they can also be harvested during the winter. Bamboo shoots are also pickled and dried for use in cooking.

Banana shallots

Banana shallots are a type of shallot. They are a cross between a regular shallot and an onion and have the best qualities from both vegetables. Banana shallots are much bigger than regular shallots and they keep the flavour and sweetness of regular shallots. You can replace this ingredient with a regular shallot if you wish to.

Chestnut mushroom

A type of mushroom that's commonly used in Western cooking. The cap of this mushroom is brown in colour. It has a delicious earthy and nutty flavour so that's why it's called "chestnut" mushroom. I use chestnut mushrooms to replace fresh shiitake mushrooms in Chinese cooking as fresh shiitake mushrooms are not easy to get hold of if you're not living in the East.

Edamame beans

Edamame beans are immature soybeans. They are a popular ingredient in Japanese cuisine but people use a lot of these in Chinese cooking. Chinese people cook edamame beans without shells. In contrast, Japanese people usually cook edamame beans with their shells.

Glutinous rice

Glutinous rice is also known as "sticky rice". It is a type of rice that has a very low amylose content and its especially sticky after it has cooked. Chinese people use glutinous rice in many different kind of dishes and for savoury foods long grain glutinous rice is usually used. There is also a short grain glutinous rice which is used in desserts.

Lily bulb

Lily bulbs are an edible bulb from the flowers you grow in your garden but this is a special type of edible lily bulb from the flower Lilium Brownil. In the East, you can generally purchase fresh lily bulbs from the market but you might only be able to get hold of dried lily bulbs. If you get the dried type, you need to rehydrate the dried lily bulb in water before cooking. I like to use room temperature water to rehydrate ingredients because warm or hot temperature water can damage the flavour of the ingredients.

Mung bean starch sheet

This ingredient is made from the starch of mung beans. It's generally used in salad dishes in Chinese cuisine. The mung bean starch product generally contains very low calories so people eat mung bean starch sheets or other kinds of mung bean products, such as cellophane noodles to try to lose weight.

Wood ear

Wood ear is a type of edible fungi and this ingredient is very popular in Chinese cuisine and Chinese medicine. You can see wood ears in hot and sour soup, stir-fries and even in dumplings or spring roll fillings. You need to rehydrate it in water before cooking it.

Chinese ham

Chinese ham is also known as *Jinhua* ham. It's a kind of dry-cured ham and I describe it to my friends as a Chinese version of prosciutto. You can use Chinese or *Jinhua* ham to make stocks, soups, stir-fries and stews.

Dried hibiscus flowers

"Roselle" is one type of hibiscus flower and in the East, people generally use this flower in hydrated form to make tea, beverages and desserts. This flower makes food and liquid turn into a beautiful ruby red colour with a refreshing sourness, so it's a popular ingredient for summer drinks in the East.

Dried jujubes

Jujube are also known as red dates or Chinese date. They are a species of Ziziphus in the buckthorn family. Jujubes are commonly used in both Chinese cuisine and Chinese medicine but Chinese people generally only use dried jujubes and not the fresh type. This ingredient can be used to make desserts, soups and for making wine. Chinese people believe jujubes can alleviate stress, anti-bacterial, anti-inflammatory, improve the wound healing process, lower the risk of cardio problems, improve the immune system and have many more health benefits, hence it's often used in Chinese medicine.

Dried osmanthus flower

Osmanthus is a tall flowering plant. The flower has a sweet and refreshing scent and due to this reason Chinese people use this flower in Chinese dessert very often.

Dried shiitake mushrooms

Dried shiitake mushrooms have a unique earthy aroma and a chewy texture. In Chinese cooking, dried shiitake mushrooms feature in many popular dishes from soups, to stews and stir-fries. When shopping for dried shiitake mushrooms, choose whole mushrooms without any broken bits. The mushroom cap should be round, thick and dark brown in colour on the outside and light yellow on the underside. This is where the flavour of shiitake mushrooms come from. Dried shiitake mushrooms need to be soaked in warm water to soften before use.

Dried tangerine peel

This refers to the sun-dried peel of the tangerine fruit. Dried tangerine peel is commonly used in Chinese and Taiwanese cuisine and in herbal medicines. The dried peel has a lovely citrus fragrance and goes well with beef, pork and duck dishes. It is also often added to desserts to enhance the flavour of the dessert.

Gammon steak

Gammon is cured ham that is very popular in Western cuisine. There are unsmoked and smoked versions and I use the smoked version to replace Chinese ham in certain dishes. Gammon steak has a smoked flavour that is quite close to Chinese ham but it's not as strong or rich.

Pickled cordia

Cordia is also known as clammy cherries, glue berries, sebesten or snotty gobbles. Pickled cordia is a very popular ingredient in Taiwan and is most commonly used in steamed seafood dishes, especially fish dishes. The pickled berries have a salty, sweet and sour flavour. When using pickled cordia in your cooking, bear in mind that other seasoning should be added sparingly.

Pickled melon

Pickled melon is basically Taiwanese-style pickled cucumber. Pickled melon tastes sweet and a little salty. You can use pickled melon to steam fish, to flavour stews and soups and even meatloaf or meatballs.

FLOURS

Glutinous rice flour

This fine white flour is commonly used for making desserts in both Taiwanese and Chinese cuisine. It is made from ground glutinous (sticky) rice and is the main ingredient for mochi and *tang yuan*, giving these desserts a lovely chewy texture. Glutinous rice flour is not the same as rice flour and cannot be used interchangeably.

Ground rice powder

Also known as *jen rou fen*, this usually comes with a five-spices flavour and can be found on the shelves in Chinese supermarkets. Chinese people use this ground rice powder to coat vegetables, for example, pumpkin or sweet potato as well as to coat meat, such as pork belly.

Potato starch

Made from potatoes, this white flour is typically used to thicken sauces and soups and to marinate meat in Chinese and Taiwanese cuisine, much like cornflour. Cornflour can be used if potato starch is not available.

Sweet potato flour

An extract of white sweet potatoes, sweet potato flour has a sweet flavour and is used in Chinese and Taiwanese cooking as a coating for deep-fried foods, desserts and soups.

HERBS AND SPICES

Chinese five-spice powder

Chinese five-spice powder is commonly made from a combination of five spices, namely star anise, cloves, Chinese cinnamon (cassia), Sichuan peppercorns and fennel seeds. In Chinese and Taiwanese cooking, five-spice powder is used when cooking fatty meats like pork and for flavouring stews.

Licorice root

Licorice comes from the root of the Glycyrrhiza glabra plant. It has a natural, earthy and mellow sweet flavour and is used in herbal medicines, cooking and sweets. Both Chinese and Taiwanese cuisine use licorice root as a spice. It helps balance the flavour of other spices used and gives the dish a natural and subtle sweetness.

Sichuan peppercorns

One of the spices in Chinese five-spice powder, Sichuan peppercorns have very strong flavour with a powerful, numbing taste. Its heat can be likened to that of very strong chillies and it can be added to give a lift to sauces and dressings.

Wolfberries

Also known as goji or goji berries, wolfberries are commonly used in herbal medicine and as a cooking spice. The Chinese also refer to them as "red diamond fruit" for their many health benefits. Dried wolfberries can be used in soups, stews and stir-fries to add a sweet flavour to the dish. They can also be added to herbal teas.

OILS, SAUCES AND PASTES

Blended sesame oil

Ideally in Chinese cooking people use white sesame oil for sauces, dressing and seasoning food. But it's not so easy to get hold of the white sesame oil (小磨香油, 白芝麻油, made with white sesame) in the city I live in so I use blended sesame oil instead. Blended sesame oil is usually made from vegetable oil mixed with toasted sesame oil. The smell and taste is a bit weaker than toasted sesame oil so when you make a sauce or use for seasoning it won't overpower other ingredients.

Chilli bean sauce

Chilli bean sauce has been called the soul of Sichuan cuisine, being the main seasoning ingredient for many popular Sichuan dishes. Also known as *dou ban jiang*, this rich, brown-coloured paste is made from fermented broad beans, soy beans, salt, rice and spices, and is a combination of spicy and salty flavours.

Dark sesame oil and sesame oil

Sesame oil is a popular ingredient in Chinese cooking and it is used in many different dishes including soups, noodles and rice dishes. Dark sesame oil is derived from toasted or roasted sesame seeds. It has a stronger flavour compared to regular sesame oil and is hence not as popular as the latter. It is mainly used in the Taiwanese three-cup dishes and sesame chicken soup. In Taiwan, it is also used in preparing confinement food as it is believed that sesame oil helps the womb contract, increases blood circulation and warms the body.

Sichuan pepper oil

Heat a wok and stir-fry 1 or 2 tablespoons of Sichuan pepper corn over medium to low heat for a couple minutes until the fragrance comes out. You don't need any oil to stir-fry the Sichuan pepper corns.

Use a mortar and pestle to grind the Sichuan peppercorn and put it into a heatproof container. Heat 4–5 tablespoons cooking oil then pour the oil into the Sichuan pepper. It's ready to use. You can store this Sichuan pepper oil in a dry and clean jar and keep in a cool, dark space for 1 month.

Chinese white sesame paste

This white sesame paste is made from toasted white sesame and some oil. You can make it at home by yourself. Simply use toasted white sesame and process with a food processor. You then slowly add vegetable oil into the mix while still processing. The mixture will reach a "paste" form then it's ready. You can store this paste in a clean and dry jar and keep it in the fridge for a month. You can purchase this white sesame past in Chinese supermarkets or if you don't want to make this sauce, you can also use tahini sauce (a white sesame sauce from the Middle East).

Rice wine and Shaoxing rice wine

Rice wine and Shaoxing rice wine are the two common types of rice wine used in Chinese and Taiwanese cooking. They are sold in bottles and are available in supermarkets and Chinese grocery stores. Rice wine (米酒) is made from regular rice and is colourless. Shaoxing rice wine (紹興酒) is made from glutinous rice and is usually brown in colour. Shaoxing rice wine has a much stronger flavour and taste of alcohol and is also a little spicy, which makes it unsuitable for many dishes, except for stronger tasting dishes such as drunken chicken, drunken prawns, Dongpo pork and other slow-cooked meat dishes. Rice wine on the other hand has a mild and refreshing taste and I use it to season many Chinese and Taiwanese dishes.

Soy sauce

There are many different types of soy sauce, and the most common types are dark soy sauce, light soy sauce and thick soy sauce. Dark soy sauce is typically used to add colour to dishes. Light soy sauce is most commonly used as a marinade, seasoning and condiment. Light soy sauce can be very salty, so use sparingly. As its name implies, thick soy sauce has a thick texture, somewhat like honey and it is both sweet and salty. It is often used to flavour stews and sauces, and can also be used as a dip.

Maltose syrup

Maltose syrup is also known as "malt syrup". This syrup gives the skin of Peking duck a layer of shining gloss, a hint of sweetness and makes the skin crispier. Maltose syrup is not as sweet as honey or other types of sugar and it's solid when it's at normal room temperature.

Sugar

WEIGHTS AND MEASURES

Quantities for this book are given in Metric and American (spoon and cup) measures. Standard spoon and cup measurements used are: 1 tsp = 5 ml, 1 Tbsp = 15 ml and 1 cup = 250 ml. All measures are level unless otherwise stated.

LIQUID AND VOLUME MEASURES

Metric	Imperial	American
5 ml	$^1/_6$ fl oz	1 tsp
10 ml	$^1/_3$ fl oz	1 dessertspoon
15 ml	$^1/_2$ fl oz	1 Tbsp
60 ml	2 fl oz	$^1/_4$ cup (4 Tbsp)
85 ml	$2^1/_2$ fl oz	$^1/_3$ cup
90 ml	3 fl oz	$^3/_8$ cup (6 Tbsp)
125 ml	4 fl oz	$^1/_2$ cup
180 ml	6 fl oz	$^3/_4$ cup
250 ml	8 fl oz	1 cup
300 ml	10 fl oz ($^1/_2$ pint)	$1^1/_4$ cups
375 ml	12 fl oz	$1^1/_2$ cups
435 ml	14 fl oz	$1^3/_4$ cups
500 ml	16 fl oz	2 cups
625 ml	20 fl oz (1 pint)	$2^1/_2$ cups
750 ml	24 fl oz ($1^1/_5$ pints)	3 cups
1 litre	32 fl oz ($1^3/_5$ pints)	4 cups
1.25 litres	40 fl oz (2 pints)	5 cups
1.5 litres	48 fl oz ($2^2/_5$ pints)	6 cups
2.5 litres	80 fl oz (4 pints)	10 cups

DRY MEASURES

Metric	Imperial
30 grams	1 ounce
45 grams	$1^1/_2$ ounces
55 grams	2 ounces
70 grams	$2^1/_2$ ounces
85 grams	3 ounces
100 grams	$3^1/_2$ ounces
110 grams	4 ounces
125 grams	$4^1/_2$ ounces
140 grams	5 ounces
280 grams	10 ounces
450 grams	16 ounces (1 pound)
500 grams	1 pound, $1^1/_2$ ounces
700 grams	$1^1/_2$ pounds
800 grams	$1^3/_4$ pounds
1 kilogram	2 pounds, 3 ounces
1.5 kilograms	3 pounds, $4^1/_2$ ounces
2 kilograms	4 pounds, 6 ounces

OVEN TEMPERATURE

	°C	°F	Gas Regulo
Very slow	120	250	1
Slow	150	300	2
Moderately slow	160	325	3
Moderate	180	350	4
Moderately hot	190/200	370/400	5/6
Hot	210/220	410/440	6/7
Very hot	230	450	8
Super hot	250/290	475/550	9/10

LENGTH

Metric	Imperial
0.5 cm	$^1/_4$ inch
1 cm	$^1/_2$ inch
1.5 cm	$^3/_4$ inch
2.5 cm	1 inch

Tsung-Yun Wan was born and raised in Taiwan. She was greatly influenced by her grandparents who were excellent cooks, and this inspired her to train as a chef in one of the top culinary schools there. She then moved to the UK, got married, and settled down in Edinburgh, Scotland, where she worked in a famous restaurant in the city until she had her first child.

To spend more time with her family, Tsung-Yun left the professional kitchen and now pursues her other passion, illustration, but her love of food is as strong as ever. The illustrations in this book were all done by her.

Since 2009, she has run her own food blog, Egg Wan's Food Odyssey. Despite her work commitments, Tsung-Yun still manages to cook wholesome, hearty meals for her family and shares the food of Taiwan and China on her blog. This is Tsung-Yun's second cookbook.

Cookbook author and food blogger Tsung-Yun Wan follows up her bestselling book *Home-style Taiwanese Cooking* with another exciting collection of 60 Chinese recipes that are sure to whet your appetite. Find mouth-watering dishes such as squid stuffed with savoury sticky rice, beef shank with spring onion pancake wraps and ginger milk curd with plum compote in this treasury of Chinese favourites.

With informative headnotes that tell the stories behind the dishes, insightful cooking tips and step-by-step photos of cooking techniques, *Home-style Chinese Cooking* will guide and inspire home cooks to prepare delicious everyday Chinese dishes in their home kitchens.

visit our website at:
www.marshallcavendish.com/genref

Marshall Cavendish Cuisine

US $34.95
ISBN 9789814751001
CAN $46.95
53495
9 789814 751001